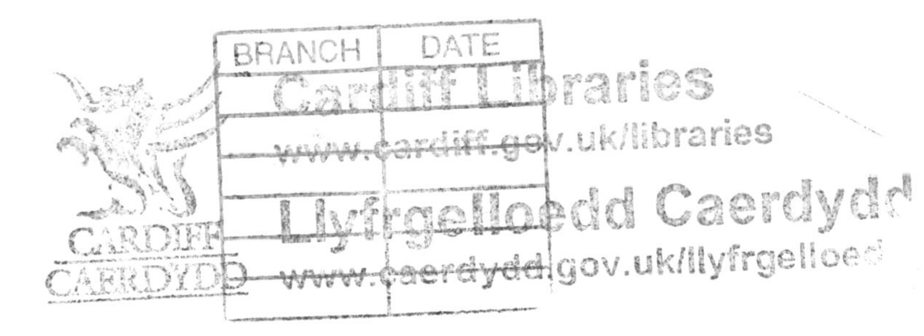
BRANCH
DATE
Cardiff Libraries
www.cardiff.gov.uk/libraries
Llyfrgelloedd Caerdydd
www.caerdydd.gov.uk/llyfrgelloed
CARDIFF
CAERDYDD

D0267794

The Railway Anthology

Compiled by

DEBORAH MANLEY

TRAILBLAZER PUBLICATIONS

The Railway Anthology
First edition: 2014

Publisher
Trailblazer Publications
The Old Manse, Tower Rd, Hindhead, Surrey, GU26 6SU, UK
www.trailblazer-guides.com

British Library Cataloguing in Publication Data
A catalogue record for this book is available from the British Library

ISBN 978-1-905864-62-1

Editors: Bryn Thomas & Nicky Slade
Layout: Bryn Thomas
Cover image: 'Express Ease' LNER Poster
© National Railway Museum / Science & Society Picture Library

DEBORAH MANLEY has lived in India, Canada, Austria and Nigeria. She worked as an editor of education books and has compiled anthologies on Malta, the Nile and the Trans-Siberian Railway. She is the author of *The Walker's Anthology* (also from Trailblazer) and co-author of the biography of the early 19th century traveller and diplomat, Henry Salt, and has also written articles for the *Guinness Book of Records 1492: The World Five Hundred Years Ago*. She now lives in Oxford.

Printed on chlorine-free paper by
booksfactory.eu

CONTENTS

CONTINENTAL EUROPE (cont'd)

ASIA

NORTH AMERICA

FURTHER AFIELD

INTRODUCTION

My first memories of rail travel are from my days as a child of the Raj.

My father was in the British army in India, training the young Indian officers who would take over from the British not many years later. We had arrived by ship at Bombay, but went on by train to Ahmednagar – my father's posting. I have little recollection of that journey, except the strange but friendly faces around us and being helped up into the train carriage and travelling through what was, to me then, strange countryside. There were other Indian train journeys during the next four years, but each runs into the next in my memory until our last train journey in India as a family. In late 1939, we set off 'home' for England from Bombay and days later arrived by ship at Marseilles for the journey north in a train across France. As we went along we could hear the distant sounds of gunfire and war – and we were thankful to reach Calais and the ship that would take us to England.

We did not spend long there for my uncle, who was in the RAF, flew government papers back from Paris over Dunkirk. He told our mother, 'You must get the children out. It cannot hold!' Before long we were on our way again, up north by train to get a ship from Liverpool to Canada and Toronto, where we were to live for the next six months or so through our first Canadian winter. From Toronto we moved to Port Hope (where the trains tooted and chuffed below us on the railway lines running alongside Lake Ontario). We then lived in Medicine Hat for a couple of years before moving further west to British Columbia and Victoria.

Our mother had what could have been an unfortunate experience at the railway station in Calgary. Accustomed to British train departures with whistles and guards waving green flags to warn the passengers that a train is about to start, she was wandering along the platform with our young brother when the train, almost silently, began to move with my sister and me on it!

'Are you supposed to be on that train?' the platform official asked. And when she said, 'Yes', he replied, 'Leave the boy and jump on. I'll pass him to you'. Somehow he did and they both joined us, flustered but safe as the train drew out of Calgary. I remember little more about that journey apart from the spectacular scenery as we passed through the Rockies.

Our father was then posted to Vienna. My mother and little brother would follow him there, but my sister and I would stay in England and go to boarding school, only spending holidays in Austria – but holidays which started and ended with the train journey across war-blackened Germany and through the Russian 'zone' of Austria to Vienna (which, as anyone who has seen *The Third Man* will know, was divided between the victors – the British, Americans, French and Russians). The Russians came through the train to check our passports and visas – in winter in fur hats, thick coats and boots, in summer in somewhat shapeless khaki 'blouses'. For the next two years, we shuttled back and forth to Vienna by train each holiday. Usually we went in a travel-weary brown train through Germany into Austria, but once we went in a smart blue train via Paris.

Then, apart from short train journeys on Britain's battered but nationalised railways, I did not often use trains until as a student I went to an International Union of Students conference in Warsaw. This time I crossed Europe by train towards the east rather than the south and could still see – in 1952 – the scars of war through countryside and cities.

And then I went on the most famous train journey of them all – on the Trans-Siberian Railway all the way from Liverpool Street Station in London to Hongkong.

'What shall we do on such a long journey?' my American friend, Barbara Shear, who came with me, asked as we prepared for the journey.

'We can read, play cards or perhaps take some knitting,' I suggested. But there was not much time for such pastimes. There was too much to see.

Some years after that, when my home town, Oxford, formed a partnership with the Russian city of Perm (just this side of the

Urals) I went by train, sometimes twice a year, to work with their emerging voluntary organisations – and people from Perm came to Oxford by train to see the evidence of what we had told them. The two cities are now twinned.

More recently, with my sister, I returned to India. She had insisted that although, or perhaps because, we were going back to India we should not go to the places where we had lived as children. She wanted the memories we had to stay as they were. She was right. Places which had been quite small in our childhood had stretched out and been magnified over the intervening decades.

The building of railways across India was probably the best thing the British did for that country. The railways link up people in reasonable comfort and efficiency from one end of the country to the other. We travelled on many of them including the luxurious 'Palace on Wheels' which was just that. In our carriage there were, I think, only four compartments. Each had two beds – not bunks but proper beds – and not even set close together. There was a toilet and shower room at each end of the carriage. Tea was brought to us in the morning and afternoon, but for other meals we got down off the train and walked along to the dining car where we were served by grandly-dressed waiters. When we stopped for a night we stayed in what had once been princely palaces which the now less well-off families were very happy to run as opulent hotels.

I have since been across Canada twice by train. Once I flew in to Ottawa to stay with friends and they put me onto the train to cross Canada. It was Christmas time and everything was both very busy and not working efficiently as usual. There was, for example, no restaurant car on the train. However, the train official took orders from us and phoned ahead to his sister and, when the train reached her station, there were sandwiches waiting to come aboard for us. Real initiative!

The next time I travelled again in winter. The snow and ice were all around and the great monster of a train trundled through the cold world, day and night, day after day from Toronto to Vancouver. I stretched my legs only occasionally, when the train stopped to pick up or put down passengers.

I have always preferred to go by train rather than by air – or even by car. And, as I hope many of the pieces in this anthology show, there are numerous benefits to travelling by rail. You have more time to look the countryside, you can read and relax, you can chat to other travellers or watch people through the windows. You get glimpses of other lives in far-off places. On that last trans-Canadian journey, at one stop an Inuit woman with her baby climbed down from the train in the middle of nowhere and there was her husband waiting to paddle her across a lake (not yet frozen solid) by the railway line to their home.

It was a scene never to be forgotten.

Deborah Manley, Oxford 2014

GREAT BRITAIN 1

Queen Victoria takes the Train, 1842

LTC Rolt

The date was Monday, 13 June 1842, and the place Slough station. A train stood at the platform headed by *Phlegethon*, one of the latest seven-foot express locomotives of the Great Western Railway. A group of black-coated officials paced the platform, nervously consulting their watches from time to time, their tall hats gleaming scarcely less brightly in the sunshine than the glossy green paint and polished metalwork of the locomotive. Mr Charles Russell, the Chairman of the Company, was there with the Secretary, Mr Saunders; so were Isambard Kingdom Brunel, the Engineer-in-Chief, and Daniel Gooch, the Superintendent of the Locomotive Department. For the train was no ordinary one and the occasion was a milestone in the history of Britain's railways. The young Queen, accompanied by her consort, was about to make her first railway journey.

Prince Albert has already used the railway several times for journeys between London and Windsor. Foreseeing that it could only be a question of time before that progressive young man persuaded Her Majesty to try the new mode of travelling, the directors had ordered to be built at Swindon a magnificent Royal Saloon. This had first been used in August 1840 by Dowager Queen Adelaide. Now, after many months of anticipation, it was standing at Slough platform, ready for the great event. The Royal Carriage was marshalled between two ordinary saloons; an open braked second-class coach was coupled next to the engine and three open carriage trucks brought up the rear.

At a little before noon the cavalcade from Windsor drove into the station yard and Charles Russell ushered the Queen into the 'splendid apartment' prepared for her, while the carriages of her attendants were loaded upon the waiting trucks. This done, she took her seat in the Royal Saloon and, punctually at noon, the train moved off with Brunel and Gooch riding on the footplate of *Phlegethon*.

Some inaccurate press reports of the occasion gave birth to the long-lived legend that Brunel actually drove the engine. But, in giving evidence before a Parliamentary Committee in the following year, the great engineer admitted with disarming frankness: 'I never dare drive an engine… because if I go upon a bit of line without anything to attract my attention I begin thinking of something else.' So it may have been as well for England and for her railways that it was Daniel Gooch and not Brunel who held the regulator on this historic occasion.

At the London end of the line, the most elaborate arrangements had been made. Says a contemporary report:

At Paddington by 11 o'clock the centre of the wide space apportioned for the arrival of trains was parted off and carpeted with a crimson carpet, which reached from one end of the platform to the other. The whole of the arrangements for the reception of the Royal party were under the superintendence of Mr Seymour Clarke, the Superintendent of the line, assisted by Supt. Collard of the Company's Police. …

Before 12 o'clock large numbers of elegantly dressed ladies consisting of the families and friends of the Directors and Officers of the Company were arranged on each side of the part apportioned for the arrival of the Royal train, and at five minutes before 12 o'clock Her Majesty's Carriage drawn by four horses arrived from the Royal Mews at Pimlico, and a few minutes afterwards a detachment of the 8th Royal Irish Hussars under the command of Capt. Sir G. Brown arrived from the Barracks at Kensington for the purpose of acting as an escort to Her Majesty.

Precisely at 25 minutes past 12 o'clock the Royal Special train entered the Terminus having performed the distance in 25 minutes, and on Her Majesty alighting she was received with the most deafening demonstrations of loyalty and affection we have ever experienced…

Over the centuries London had welcomed many a king and queen, but this occasion was unique. Never before had a reigning

I am going to design a station, in a great hurry, after

sovereign made such an entry into the capital city. No one of those who cheered the young Queen could possibly have realized how fitting the occasion was; for Victoria's long reign would give a name to an age, an age to be forever preeminently associated with steam power and steam railways.

(From *Victorian Engineering: A fascinating story of invention and achievement;* Penguin, 1970, © LTC Rolt)

The Excursion Train to London, 1851

THOMAS HARDY

Having lost Car'line to the fiddler, Mop, Ned makes a life for himself in London. Soon discarded by Mop, Car'line writes to Ned who decides to take her back if she will come to him in London and become his wife ...

He added that the request for her to come to him was a less one to make than it would have been when he first left Stickleford, or even a few months ago; for the new railway into South Wessex was now open, and there had just begun to be run wonderfully contrived special trains, called excursion-trains, on account of the Great Exhibition; so that she could come up easily alone.

She said in her reply how good it was of him to treat her so generously, after her hot and cold treatment of him; that though she felt frightened at the magnitude of the journey, and was never as yet in a railway-train, having only seen one pass at a distance, she embraced his offer with all her heart; and would, indeed, own to him how sorry she was, and beg his pardon, and try to be a good wife always, and make up for lost time.

The remaining details of when and where were soon settled, Car'line informing him, for her ready identification in the crowd, that she would be wearing 'my new sprigged-laylock cotton gown,' and Ned gaily responding that, having married her the morning after her arrival, he would make a day of it by taking her to the Exhibition. One early summer afternoon, accordingly, he came from his place of work, and hastened towards Waterloo Station to meet her. It was as wet and chilly as an English June

my own fancy ... with engineering roofs, etc.
ISAMBARD KINGDOM BRUNEL

day can occasionally be, but as he waited on the platform in the drizzle he glowed inwardly, and seemed to have something to live for again.

The 'excursion-train' – an absolutely new departure in the history of travel – was still a novelty on the Wessex line, and probably everywhere. Crowds of people had flocked to all the stations on the way up to witness the unwonted sight of so long a train's passage, even where they did not take advantage of the opportunity it offered. The seats for the humbler class of travellers in these early experiments in steam-locomotion, were open trucks, without any protection whatever from the wind and rain; and damp weather having set in with the afternoon, the unfortunate occupants of these vehicles were, on the train drawing up at the London terminus, found to be in a pitiable condition from their long journey; blue-faced, stiff-necked, sneezing, rain-beaten, chilled to the marrow, many of the men being hatless; in fact, they resembled people who had been out all night in an open boat on a rough sea, rather than inland excursionists for pleasure. The women had in some degree protected themselves by turning up the skirts of their gowns over their heads, but as by this arrangement they were additionally exposed about the hips, they were all more or less in a sorry plight.

In the bustle and crush of alighting forms of both sexes which followed the entry of the huge concatenation into the station, Ned Hipcroft soon discerned the slim little figure his eye was in search of, in the sprigged lilac, as described. She came up to him with a frightened smile – still pretty, though so damp, weather-beaten, and shivering from long exposure to the wind.

'O Ned!' she sputtered, 'I – I – ' He clasped her in his arms and kissed her, whereupon she burst into a flood of tears.

'You are wet, my poor dear! I hope you'll not get cold,' he said. And surveying her and her multifarious surrounding packages, he noticed that by the hand she led a toddling child – a little girl of three or so – whose hood was as clammy and tender face as blue as those of the other travellers.

'Who is this – somebody you know?' asked Ned curiously.

'Yes, Ned. She's mine.'

Isambard Kingdom Brunel ... Anyone who builds a railway can't go any further must

'Yours?'

'Yes – my own!'

'Your own child?'

'Yes!'

'Well – as God's in-'

'Ned, I didn't name it in my letter, because, you see, it would have been so hard to explain! I thought that when we met I could tell you how she happened to be born, so much better than in writing! I hope you'll excuse it this once, dear Ned, and not scold me, now I've come so many, many miles!'

'This means Mr. Mop Ollamoor, I reckon!' said Hipcroft, gazing palely at them from the distance of the yard or two to which he had withdrawn with a start.

Car'line gasped. 'But he's been gone away for years!' she supplicated. 'And I never had a young man before! And I was so unlucky to be catched the first time, though some of the girls down there go on like anything!'

(From *The Fiddler of the Reels*; Scribner's Magazine, 1893)

A Question of Class, 1862

Anthony Trollope

In class conscious Britain of the 19th century the distinctions were clear cut on the railway system...

[Mr. Dockwrath] had left Leeds at ten, and Mr. Moulder had come down in the same omnibus to the station, and was travelling in the same train in a first-class carriage. Mr. Moulder was a man who despised the second-class, and was not slow to say so before other commercials who travelled at a cheaper rate than he did. 'Hubbles and Grease,' he said, 'allowed him respectably, in order that he might go about their business respectable; and he wasn't going to give the firm a bad name by being seen in a second-class carriage, although the difference would go into his own pocket. That wasn't the way he had begun, and that wasn't the way he was going to end.' He said nothing to Mr. Dockwrath

and then builds a steamship when he gets to Bristol and be a good chap. Fergus Henderson

in the morning, merely bowing in answer to that gentleman's salutation. 'Hope you were comfortable last night in the back drawing-room,' said Mr. Dockwrath; but Mr. Moulder in reply only looked at him.

At the Mansfield station, Mr. Kantwise, with his huge wooden boxes, appeared on the platform, and he got into the same carriage with Mr. Dockwrath. He had come on by a night train, and had been doing a stroke of business that morning. 'Well, Kantwise,' Moulder holloaed out from his warm, well-padded seat, 'doing it cheap and nasty, eh?'

'Not at all nasty, Mr. Moulder,' said the other. 'And I find myself among as respectable a class of society in the second-class as you do in the first; quite so; – and perhaps a little better,' Mr. Kantwise added, as he took his seat immediately opposite to Mr. Dockwrath.

(From *Orley Farm*; 1862)

The Last Praerailroadites, 1863

William Makepeace Thackeray

The coming of the railways heralded a new age – another world – not just a new stage in life as Thackeray emphatically points out, feeling that he was one of the last of those from that earlier age...

O pity! The vision has disappeared off the silver, the images of youth and the past are vanishing away! We who have lived before railways were made, belong to another world. In how many hours could the Prince of Wales drive from Brighton to London, with a light carriage built expressly, and relays of horses longing to gallop the next stage? Do you remember Sir Somebody, the coachman of the Age, who took our half-crown so affably? It was only yesterday; but what a gulf between now and then! THEN was the old world. Stage-coaches, more or less swift, riding-horses, pack-horses, highwaymen, knights in armour, Norman invaders, Roman legions, Druids, Ancient Britons painted blue, and so forth – all these belong to the old period. I will

The press, the machine, the railway, the telegraph are yet dared to draw.

concede a halt in the midst of it, and allow that gunpowder and printing tended to modernize the world. But your railroad starts the new era, and we of a certain age belong to the new time and the old one. We are of the time of chivalry as well as the Black Prince or Sir Walter Manny. We are of the age of steam. We have stepped out of the old world on to 'Brunel's' vast deck, and across the waters *ingens patet tellus*. Towards what new continent are we wending? to what new laws, new manners, new politics, vast new expanses of liberties unknown as yet, or only surmised? I used to know a man who had invented a flying-machine. 'Sir,' he would say, 'give me but five hundred pounds, and I will make it. It is so simple of construction that I tremble daily lest some other person should light upon and patent my discovery.' Perhaps faith was wanting; perhaps the five hundred pounds. He is dead, and somebody else must make the flying-machine. But that will only be a step forward on the journey already begun since we quitted the old world. There it lies on the other side of yonder embankments. You young folks have never seen it; and Waterloo is to you no more than Agincourt, and George IV. than Sardanapalus. We elderly people have lived in that praerailroad world, which has passed into limbo and vanished from under us. I tell you it was firm under our feet once, and not long ago. They have raised those railroad embankments up, and shut off the old world that was behind them. Climb up that bank on which the irons are laid, and look to the other side – it is gone. There IS no other side. Try and catch yesterday. Where is it? Here is a *Times* newspaper, dated Monday 26th, and this is Tuesday 27th. Suppose you deny there was such a day as yesterday?

We who lived before railways, and survive out of the ancient world, are like Father Noah and his family out of the Ark. The children will gather round and say to us patriarchs, 'Tell us, grandpapa, about the old world.' And we shall mumble our old stories; and we shall drop off one by one; and there will be fewer and fewer of us, and these very old and feeble. There will be but ten praerailroadites left: then three then two – then one – then 0! If the hippopotamus had the least sensibility (of which I cannot

premises whose thousand-year conclusion no one has
FRIEDRICH NIETZSCHE

trace any signs either in his hide or his face), I think he would go down to the bottom of his tank, and never come up again. Does he not see that he belongs to bygone ages, and that his great hulking barrel of a body is out of place in these times? What has he in common with the brisk young life surrounding him? In the watches of the night, when the keepers are asleep, when the birds are on one leg, when even the little armadillo is quiet, and the monkeys have ceased their chatter, – he, I mean the hippopotamus, and the elephant, and the long-necked giraffe, perhaps may lay their heads together and have a colloquy about the great silent antediluvian world which they remember, where mighty monsters floundered through the ooze, crocodiles basked on the banks, and dragons darted out of the caves and waters before men were made to slay them. We who lived before railways are antediluvians – we must pass away. We are growing scarcer every day; and old – old – very old relicts of the times when George was still fighting the Dragon.

(From *Roundabout Papers, De Juventute*; 1863)

The Speculators, 1864

William Makepeace Thackeray

The night was stormy and dark,
The town was shut up in sleep:
Only those were abroad who were out on a lark,
Or those who'd no beds to keep.

I pass'd through the lonely street,
The wind did sing and blow;
I could hear the policeman's feet
Clapping to and fro.

There stood a potato-man
In the midst of all the wet;
He stood with his 'tato-can
In the lonely Hay-market.

The Internet, like the steam engine, is a technological

Two gents of dismal mien,
And dank and greasy rags,
Came out of a shop for gin,
Swaggering over the flags:

Swaggering over the stones,
These shabby bucks did walk;
And I went and followed those seedy ones,
And listened to their talk.

Was I sober or awake?
Could I believe my ears?
Those dismal beggars spake
Of nothing but railroad shares.

I wondered more and more:
Says one – 'Good friend of mine,
How many shares have you wrote for,
In the Diddlesex Junction line?'

'I wrote for twenty,' says Jim,
'But they wouldn't give me one;'
His comrade straight rebuked him
For the folly he had done:

'O Jim, you are unawares
Of the ways of this bad town;
I always write for five hundred shares,
And THEN they put me down.'

'And yet you got no shares,'
Says Jim, 'for all your boast;'
'I WOULD have wrote,' says Jack, 'but where
Was the penny to pay the post?'

'I lost, for I couldn't pay
That first instalment up;

But here's 'taters smoking hot – I say,
Let's stop, my boy, and sup.'

And at this simple feast
The while they did regale,
I drew each ragged capitalist
Down on my left thumbnail.

Their talk did me perplex,
All night I tumbled and tost,
And thought of railroad specs,
And how money was won and lost.

'Bless railroads everywhere,'
I said, 'and the world's advance;
Bless every railroad share
In Italy, Ireland, France;
For never a beggar need now despair,
And every rogue has a chance.'

(From *The Works of William Makepeace Thackeray*; Harper & Bros, 1899)

The Looking-Glass Train, 1871

Lewis Carroll

'Tickets, please!' said the Guard, putting his head in at the window. In a moment everybody was holding out a ticket: they were about the same size as the people, and quite seemed to fill the carriage.

'Now then! Show your ticket, child!' the Guard went on, looking angrily at Alice. And a great many voices all said together ('like the chorus of a song,' thought Alice), 'Don't keep him waiting, child! Why, his time is worth a thousand pounds a minute!'

'I'm afraid I haven't got one,' Alice said in a frightened tone: 'there wasn't a ticket-office where I came from.' And again the

My first career ambitions involved turning into a boy;

chorus of voices went on. 'There wasn't room for one where she came from. The land there is worth a thousand pounds an inch!'

'Don't make excuses,' said the Guard: 'you should have bought one from the engine-driver.' And once more the chorus of voices went on with 'The man that drives the engine. Why, the smoke alone is worth a thousand pounds a puff!'

Alice thought to herself, 'Then there's no use in speaking.' The voices didn't join in this time, as she hadn't spoken, but to her great surprise, they all THOUGHT in chorus (I hope you understand what THINKING IN CHORUS means – for I must confess that I don't), 'Better say nothing at all. Language is worth a thousand pounds a word!'

'I shall dream about a thousand pounds tonight, I know I shall!' thought Alice.

All this time the Guard was looking at her, first through a telescope, then through a microscope, and then through an opera-glass. At last he said, 'You're travelling the wrong way,' and shut up the window and went away.

'So young a child,' said the gentleman sitting opposite to her (he was dressed in white paper), 'ought to know which way she's going, even if she doesn't know her own name!'

A Goat, that was sitting next to the gentleman in white, shut his eyes and said in a loud voice, 'She ought to know her way to the ticket-office, even if she doesn't know her alphabet!'

There was a Beetle sitting next to the Goat (it was a very queer carriage-full of passengers altogether), and, as the rule seemed to be that they should all speak in turn, HE went on with 'She'll have to go back from here as luggage!'

Alice couldn't see who was sitting beyond the Beetle, but a hoarse voice spoke next. 'Change engines – ' it said, and was obliged to leave off.

'It sounds like a horse,' Alice thought to herself. And an extremely small voice, close to her ear, said, 'You might make a joke on that – something about 'horse' and 'hoarse,' you know.'

I intended to be either a railway guard or a knight errant.
HILARY MANTEL

Then a very gentle voice in the distance said, 'She must be labelled 'Lass, with care,' you know – '

And after that other voices went on ('What a number of people there are in the carriage!' thought Alice), saying, 'She must go by post, as she's got a head on her – ' 'She must be sent as a message by the telegraph – ' 'She must draw the train herself the rest of the way – ' and so on.

But the gentleman dressed in white paper leaned forwards and whispered in her ear, 'Never mind what they all say, my dear, but take a return-ticket every time the train stops.'

'Indeed I shan't!' Alice said rather impatiently. 'I don't belong to this railway journey at all – I was in a wood just now – and I wish I could get back there.'

'You might make a joke on THAT,' said the little voice close to her ear: 'something about 'you WOULD if you could,' you know.'

'Don't tease so,' said Alice, looking about in vain to see where the voice came from; 'if you're so anxious to have a joke made, why don't you make one yourself?'

The little voice sighed deeply: it was VERY unhappy, evidently, and Alice would have said something pitying to comfort it, 'If it would only sigh like other people!' she thought. But this was such a wonderfully small sigh, that she wouldn't have heard it at all, if it hadn't come QUITE close to her ear. The consequence of this was that it tickled her ear very much, and quite took off her thoughts from the unhappiness of the poor little creature.

'I know you are a friend,' the little voice went on; 'a dear friend, and an old friend. And you won't hurt me, though I AM an insect.'

'What kind of insect?' Alice inquired a little anxiously. What she really wanted to know was, whether it could sting or not, but she thought this wouldn't be quite a civil question to ask.

'What, then you don't – ' the little voice began, when it was drowned by a shrill scream from the engine, and everybody jumped up in alarm, Alice among the rest.

The Horse, who had put his head out of the window, quietly drew it in and said, 'It's only a brook we have to jump over.' Everybody seemed satisfied with this, though Alice felt a little nervous at the idea of trains jumping at all. 'However, it'll take us into the Fourth Square, that's some comfort!' she said to herself. In another moment she felt the carriage rise straight up into the air, and in her fright she caught at the thing nearest to her hand, which happened to be the Goat's beard.

(From *Through the Looking-Glass*; 1871)

The Railway comes to Middlemarch, 1871

George Eliot

As he said, 'Business breeds.' And one form of business which was beginning to breed just then was the construction of railways. A projected line was to run through Lowick parish where the cattle had hitherto grazed in a peace unbroken by astonishment; and thus it happened that the infant struggles of the railway system entered into the affairs of Caleb Garth, and determined the course of this history with regard to two persons who were dear to him. The submarine railway may have its difficulties; but the bed of the sea is not divided among various landed proprietors with claims for damages not only measurable but sentimental. In the hundred to which Middlemarch belonged railways were as exciting a topic as the Reform Bill or the imminent horrors of Cholera, and those who held the most decided views on the subject were women and landholders. Women both old and young regarded travelling by steam as presumptuous and dangerous, and argued against it by saying that nothing should induce them to get into a railway carriage; while proprietors, differing from each other in their arguments as much as Mr. Solomon Featherstone differed from Lord Medlicote, were yet unanimous in the opinion that in selling land, whether to the Enemy of mankind or to a company obliged to purchase, these pernicious agencies must be made to pay a very high price to landowners for permission to injure mankind.

20 years ago on a train ride from Manhattan to Hollywood.
Walt Disney

But the slower wits, such as Mr. Solomon and Mrs. Waule, who both occupied land of their own, took a long time to arrive at this conclusion, their minds halting at the vivid conception of what it would be to cut the Big Pasture in two, and turn it into three-cornered bits, which would be 'nohow;' while accommodation bridges and high payments were remote and incredible.

'The cows will all cast their calves, brother,' said Mrs. Waule, in a tone of deep melancholy, 'if the railway comes across the Near Close; and I shouldn't wonder at the mare too, if she was in foal. It's a poor tale if a widow's property is to be spaded away, and the law say nothing to it. What's to hinder 'em from cutting right and left if they begin? It's well known, *I* can't fight.'

'The best way would be to say nothing, and set somebody on to send 'em away with a flea in their ear, when they came spying and measuring,' said Solomon. 'Folks did that about Brassing, by what I can understand. It's all a pretence, if the truth was known, about their being forced to take one way. Let 'em go cutting in another parish. And I don't believe in any pay to make amends for bringing a lot of ruffians to trample your crops. Where's a company's pocket?'

'Brother Peter, God forgive him, got money out of a company,' said Mrs. Waule. 'But that was for the manganese. That wasn't for railways to blow you to pieces right and left.'

'Well, there's this to be said, Jane,' Mr. Solomon concluded, lowering his voice in a cautious manner – 'the more spokes we put in their wheel, the more they'll pay us to let 'em go on, if they must come whether or not.'

This reasoning of Mr. Solomon's was perhaps less thorough than he imagined, his cunning bearing about the same relation to the course of railways as the cunning of a diplomatist bears to the general chill or catarrh of the solar system. But he set about acting on his views in a thoroughly diplomatic manner, by stimulating suspicion. His side of Lowick was the most remote from the village, and the houses of the labouring people were either lone cottages or were collected in a hamlet called Frick, where a water-

The aristocrats ... generally hated the whole concept of the to move about and not always

mill and some stone-pits made a little centre of slow, heavy-shouldered industry.

In the absence of any precise idea as to what railways were, public opinion in Frick was against them; for the human mind in that grassy corner had not the proverbial tendency to admire the unknown, holding rather that it was likely to be against the poor man, and that suspicion was the only wise attitude with regard to it. ... Thus the mind of Frick was exactly of the sort for Mr. Solomon Featherstone to work upon, he having more plenteous ideas of the same order, with a suspicion of heaven and earth which was better fed and more entirely at leisure. Solomon was overseer of the roads at that time, and on his slow-paced cob often took his rounds by Frick to look at the workmen getting the stones there, pausing with a mysterious deliberation, which might have misled you into supposing that he had some other reason for staying than the mere want of impulse to move. ... One day, however, he got into a dialogue with Hiram Ford, a wagoner, in which he himself contributed information. He wished to know whether Hiram had seen fellows with staves and instruments spying about: they called themselves railroad people, but there was no telling what they were or what they meant to do. The least they pretended was that they were going to cut Lowick Parish into sixes and sevens.

'Why, there'll be no stirrin' from one pla-ace to another,' said Hiram, thinking of his wagon and horses.

'Not a bit,' said Mr. Solomon. 'And cutting up fine land such as this parish! Let 'em go into Tipton, say I. But there's no knowing what there is at the bottom of it. Traffic is what they put for'ard; but it's to do harm to the land and the poor man in the long-run.'

'Why, they're Lunnon chaps, I reckon,' said Hiram, who had a dim notion of London as a centre of hostility to the country.

'Ay, to be sure. And in some parts against Brassing, by what I've heard say, the folks fell on 'em when they were spying, and broke their peep-holes as they carry, and drove 'em away, so as they knew better than come again.'

train on the basis that it would encourage the lower classes be available. TERRY PRATCHETT

'It war good foon, I'd be bound,' said Hiram, whose fun was much restricted by circumstances.

'Well, I wouldn't meddle with 'em myself,' said Solomon. 'But some say this country's seen its best days, and the sign is, as it's being overrun with these fellows trampling right and left, and wanting to cut it up into railways; and all for the big traffic to swallow up the little, so as there shan't be a team left on the land, nor a whip to crack.'

☆ ☆ ☆

One morning, not long after that interview between Mr. Farebrother and Mary Garth, in which she confessed to him her feeling for Fred Vincy, it happened that her father had some business which took him to Yoddrell's farm in the direction of Frick: it was to measure and value an outlying piece of land belonging to Lowick Manor, which Caleb expected to dispose of advantageously for Dorothea (it must be confessed that his bias was towards getting the best possible terms from railroad companies). He put up his gig at Yoddrell's, and in walking with his assistant and measuring-chain to the scene of his work, he encountered the party of the company's agents, who were adjusting their spirit-level. After a little chat he left them, observing that by-and-by they would reach him again where he was going to measure. It was one of those gray mornings after light rains, which become delicious about twelve o'clock, when the clouds part a little, and the scent of the earth is sweet along the lanes and by the hedgerows.

The scent would have been sweeter to Fred Vincy, who was coming along the lanes on horseback, if his mind had not been worried by unsuccessful efforts to imagine what he was to do, with his father on one side expecting him straightway to enter the Church, with Mary on the other threatening to forsake him if he did enter it, and with the working-day world showing no eager need whatever of a young gentleman without capital and generally unskilled. It was the harder to Fred's disposition because his father, satisfied that he was no longer rebellious, was in good humour with him, and had sent him on this pleasant ride to see after some greyhounds. Even when he had fixed on what he

It is arguable whether the human race have been gainers

should do, there would be the task of telling his father. But it must be admitted that the fixing, which had to come first, was the more difficult task: – what secular avocation on earth was there for a young man (whose friends could not get him an 'appointment') which was at once gentlemanly, lucrative, and to be followed without special knowledge? Riding along the lanes by Frick in this mood, and slackening his pace while he reflected whether he should venture to go round by Lowick Parsonage to call on Mary, he could see over the hedges from one field to another. Suddenly a noise roused his attention, and on the far side of a field on his left hand he could see six or seven men in smock-frocks with hay-forks in their hands making an offensive approach towards the four railway agents who were facing them, while Caleb Garth and his assistant were hastening across the field to join the threatened group. Fred, delayed a few moments by having to find the gate, could not gallop up to the spot before the party in smock-frocks, whose work of turning the hay had not been too pressing after swallowing their mid-day beer, were driving the men in coats before them with their hay-forks; while Caleb Garth's assistant, a lad of seventeen, who had snatched up the spirit-level at Caleb's order, had been knocked down and seemed to be lying helpless. The coated men had the advantage as runners, and Fred covered their retreat by getting in front of the smock-frocks and charging them suddenly enough to throw their chase into confusion. 'What do you confounded fools mean?' shouted Fred, pursuing the divided group in a zigzag, and cutting right and left with his whip. 'I'll swear to every one of you before the magistrate. You've knocked the lad down and killed him, for what I know. You'll every one of you be hanged at the next assizes, if you don't mind,' said Fred, who afterwards laughed heartily as he remembered his own phrases.

The labourers had been driven through the gate-way into their hay-field, and Fred had checked his horse, when Hiram Ford, observing himself at a safe challenging distance, turned back and shouted a defiance which he did not know to be Homeric.

'Yo're a coward, yo are. Yo git off your horse, young measter, and I'll have a round wi' ye, I wull. Yo daredn't come on wi'out

by the march of science beyond the steam engine.
WINSTON CHURCHILL

your hoss an' whip. I'd soon knock the breath out on ye, I would.'

'Wait a minute, and I'll come back presently, and have a round with you all in turn, if you like,' said Fred, who felt confidence in his power of boxing with his dearly beloved brethren. But just now he wanted to hasten back to Caleb and the prostrate youth.

The lad's ankle was strained, and he was in much pain from it, but he was no further hurt, and Fred placed him on the horse that he might ride to Yoddrell's and be taken care of there.

'Let them put the horse in the stable, and tell the surveyors they can come back for their traps,' said Fred. 'The ground is clear now.'

'No, no,' said Caleb, 'here's a breakage. They'll have to give up for to-day, and it will be as well. Here, take the things before you on the horse, Tom. They'll see you coming, and they'll turn back.'

'I'm glad I happened to be here at the right moment, Mr. Garth,' said Fred, as Tom rode away. 'No knowing what might have happened if the cavalry had not come up in time.'

'Ay, ay, it was lucky,' said Caleb, speaking rather absently, and looking towards the spot where he had been at work at the moment of interruption. 'But – deuce take it – this is what comes of men being fools – I'm hindered of my day's work. I can't get along without somebody to help me with the measuring-chain. However!' He was beginning to move towards the spot with a look of vexation, as if he had forgotten Fred's presence, but suddenly he turned round and said quickly, 'What have you got to do to-day, young fellow?'

'Nothing, Mr. Garth. I'll help you with pleasure – can I?' said Fred, with a sense that he should be courting Mary when he was helping her father.

'Well, you mustn't mind stooping and getting hot.'

'I don't mind anything. Only I want to go first and have a round with that hulky fellow who turned to challenge me. It would be a good lesson for him. I shall not be five minutes.'

Science owes more to the steam engine than

'Nonsense!' said Caleb, with his most peremptory intonation. 'I shall go and speak to the men myself. It's all ignorance. Somebody has been telling them lies. The poor fools don't know any better.'

'I shall go with you, then,' said Fred.

'No, no; stay where you are. I don't want your young blood. I can take care of myself.'

Caleb was a powerful man and knew little of any fear except the fear of hurting others and the fear of having to speechify. But he felt it his duty at this moment to try and give a little harangue. There was a striking mixture in him – which came from his having always been a hard-working man himself – of rigorous notions about workmen and practical indulgence towards them. To do a good day's work and to do it well, he held to be part of their welfare, as it was the chief part of his own happiness; but he had a strong sense of fellowship with them. When he advanced towards the labourers they had not gone to work again, but were standing in that form of rural grouping which consists in each turning a shoulder towards the other, at a distance of two or three yards. They looked rather sulkily at Caleb, who walked quickly with one hand in his pocket and the other thrust between the buttons of his waistcoat, and had his every-day mild air when he paused among them.

'Why, my lads, how's this?' he began, taking as usual to brief phrases, which seemed pregnant to himself, because he had many thoughts lying under them, like the abundant roots of a plant that just manages to peep above the water. 'How came you to make such a mistake as this? Somebody has been telling you lies. You thought those men up there wanted to do mischief.'

'Aw!' was the answer, dropped at intervals by each according to his degree of unreadiness.

'Nonsense! No such thing! They're looking out to see which way the railroad is to take. Now, my lads, you can't hinder the railroad: it will be made whether you like it or not. And if you go fighting against it, you'll get yourselves into trouble. The law gives those men leave to come here on the land. The owner has

the steam engine owes to science. LJ HENDERSON

nothing to say against it, and if you meddle with them you'll have to do with the constable and Justice Blakesley, and with the handcuffs and Middlemarch jail. And you might be in for it now, if anybody informed against you.'

Caleb paused here, and perhaps the greatest orator could not have chosen either his pause or his images better for the occasion.

'But come, you didn't mean any harm. Somebody told you the railroad was a bad thing. That was a lie. It may do a bit of harm here and there, to this and to that; and so does the sun in heaven. But the railway's a good thing.'

'Aw! good for the big folks to make money out on,' said old Timothy Cooper, who had stayed behind turning his hay while the others had been gone on their spree; – 'I'n seen lots o' things turn up sin' I war a young un – the war an' the peace, and the canells, an' the oald King George, an' the Regen', an' the new King George, an' the new un as has got a new ne-ame – an' it's been all aloike to the poor mon. What's the canells been t' him? They'n brought him neyther me-at nor be-acon, nor wage to lay by, if he didn't save it wi' clemmin' his own inside. Times ha' got wusser for him sin' I war a young un. An' so it'll be wi' the railroads. They'll on'y leave the poor mon furder behind. But them are fools as meddle, and so I told the chaps here. This is the big folks's world, this is. But yo're for the big folks, Muster Garth, yo are.'

(From *Middlemarch*; 1874)

Journey's End, 1876

Anthony Trollope

Ferdinand Lopez is a city speculator who has overextended himself and now faces financial ruin. His last-ditch attempt to solve his financial problems by leaving his wife and running away to Central America with a wealthy socialite, Lizzie Eustace, fails and so he is forced to pursue a more drastic plan ...

Early on the following morning he was up, and before he left his room he kissed his wife. 'Good-bye, old girl,' he said; 'don't be down-hearted.'

When steam first began to pump and wheels go round, life of man run in harmony with the steam engine, and

'If you have anything before you to do, I will not be down-hearted,' she said.

'I shall have something to do before night, I think. Tell your father, when you see him, that I will not trouble him here much longer. But tell him, also, that I have no thanks to give him for his hospitality.'

'I will not tell him that, Ferdinand.'

'He shall know it, though. But I do not mean to be cross to you. Good-bye, love.' Then he stooped over her and kissed her again; – and so he took his leave of her.

It was raining hard, and when he got into the street he looked about for a cab, but there was none to be found. In Baker Street he got an omnibus which took him down to the underground railway, and by that he went to Gower Street. Through the rain he walked up to the Euston Station, and there he ordered breakfast. Could he have a mutton chop and some tea? And he was very particular that the mutton chop should be well cooked. He was a good-looking man, of fashionable appearance, and the young lady who attended him noticed him and was courteous to him. He condescended even to have a little light conversation with her, and, on the whole, he seemed to enjoy his breakfast. 'Upon my word, I should like to breakfast here every day of my life,' he said. The young lady assured him that, as far as she could see, there was no objection to such an arrangement. 'Only it's a bore, you know, coming out in the rain when there are no cabs,' he said. Then there were various little jokes between them, till the young lady was quite impressed with the gentleman's pleasant affability.

After a while he went back into the hall and took a first-class return ticket, not for Birmingham, but for the Tenway Junction. It is quite unnecessary to describe the Tenway Junction, as everybody knows it. From this spot, some six or seven miles distant from London, lines diverge east, west, and north, north-east, and north-west, round the metropolis in every direction, and with direct communication with every other line in and out of London. It is a marvellous place, quite unintelligible to the uninitiated,

what are called business habits were intended to make the his movement rival the train in punctuality. GW Russell

and yet daily used by thousands who only know that when they get there, they are to do what some one tells them. The space occupied by the convergent rails seems to be sufficient for a large farm. And these rails always run one into another with sloping points, and cross passages, and mysterious meandering sidings, till it seems to the thoughtful stranger to be impossible that the best trained engine should know its own line. Here and there and around there is ever a wilderness of waggons, some loaded, some empty, some smoking with close-packed oxen, and others furlongs in length black with coals, which look as though they had been stranded there by chance, and were never destined to get again into the right path of traffic. Not a minute passes without a train going here or there, some rushing by without noticing Tenway in the least, crashing through like flashes of substantial lightning, and others stopping, disgorging and taking up passengers by the hundreds. Men and women, – especially the men, for the women knowing their ignorance are generally willing to trust to the pundits of the place, – look doubtful, uneasy, and bewildered. But they all do get properly placed and unplaced, so that the spectator at last acknowledges that over all this apparent chaos there is presiding a great genius of order. From dusky morn to dark night, and indeed almost throughout the night, the air is loaded with a succession of shrieks. The theory goes that each separate shriek, – if there can be any separation where the sound is so nearly continuous, – is a separate notice to separate ears of the coming or going of a separate train. The stranger, as he speculates on these pandemoniac noises, is able to realise the idea that were they discontinued the excitement necessary for the minds of the pundits might be lowered, and that activity might be lessened, and evil results might follow. But he cannot bring himself to credit that theory of individual notices.

At Tenway Junction there are half-a-dozen long platforms, on which men and women and luggage are crowded. On one of these for a while Ferdinand Lopez walked backwards and forwards as though waiting for the coming of some especial train. The crowd is ever so great that a man might be supposed to walk

The world's oldest working railway, built

there from morning to night without exciting special notice. But the pundits are very clever, and have much experience in men and women. A well-taught pundit, who has exercised authority for a year or two at such a station as that of Tenway, will know within a minute of the appearance of each stranger what is his purpose there, – whether he be going or has just come, whether he is himself on the way or waiting for others, whether he should be treated with civility or with some curt command, – so that if his purport be honest all necessary assistance may be rendered him. As Lopez was walking up and down, with smiling face and leisurely pace, now reading an advertisement and now watching the contortions of some amazed passenger, a certain pundit asked him his business. He was waiting, he said, for a train from Liverpool, intending, when his friend arrived, to go with him to Dulwich by a train which went round the west of London. It was all feasible, and the pundit told him that the stopping train from Liverpool was due there in six minutes, but that the express from the north would pass first. Lopez thanked the pundit and gave him sixpence, – which made the pundit suspicious. A pundit hopes to be paid when he handles luggage, but has no such expectation when he merely gives information.

The pundit still had his eye on our friend when the shriek and the whirr of the express from the north was heard. Lopez walked quickly up towards the edge of the platform, when the pundit followed him, telling him that this was not his train. Lopez then ran a few yards along the platform, not noticing the man, reaching a spot that was unoccupied; – and there he stood fixed. And as he stood the express flashed by. 'I am fond of seeing them pass like that,' said Lopez to the man who had followed him.

'But you shouldn't do it, sir,' said the suspicious pundit. 'No one isn't allowed to stand near like that. The very hair of it might take you off your legs when you're not used to it.'

'All right, old fellow,' said Lopez, retreating. The next train was the Liverpool train; and it seemed that our friend's friend

in 1758, is the Middleton Railway in Leeds.

had not come, for when the Liverpool passengers had cleared themselves off, he was still walking up and down the platform. 'He'll come by the next,' said Lopez to the pundit, who now followed him about and kept an eye on him.

'There ain't another from Liverpool stopping here till the 2.20,' said the pundit. 'You had better come again if you mean to meet him by that.'

'He has come on part of the way, and will reach this by some other train,' said Lopez.

'There ain't nothing he can come by,' said the pundit. 'Gentlemen can't wait here all day, sir. The horders is against waiting on the platform.'

'All right,' said Lopez, moving away as though to make his exit through the station.

Now Tenway Junction is so big a place, and so scattered, that it is impossible that all the pundits should by any combined activity maintain to the letter that order of which our special pundit had spoken. Lopez, departing from the platform which he had hitherto occupied, was soon to be seen on another, walking up and down, and again waiting. But the old pundit had had his eye upon him, and had followed him round. At that moment there came a shriek louder than all the other shrieks, and the morning express down from Euston to Inverness was seen coming round the curve at a thousand miles an hour. Lopez turned round and looked at it, and again walked towards the edge of the platform. But now it was not exactly the edge that he neared, but a descent to a pathway, – an inclined plane leading down to the level of the rails, and made there for certain purposes of traffic. As he did so the pundit called to him, and then made a rush at him, – for our friend's back was turned to the coming train. But Lopez heeded not the call, and the rush was too late. With quick, but still with gentle and apparently unhurried steps, he walked down before the flying engine – and in a moment had been knocked into bloody atoms.

(From *The Prime Minister*; 1876)

Everything one does in life, even love, occurs in an

The Tay Bridge Disaster, 1879

WILLIAM McGONAGALL

Written in 1880 to commemorate one of the worst railway accidents in the history of railways – the collapse of the first Tay Bridge on the night of 28th December 1879 – McGonagall's poem is similarly infamous, being the work of a man widely acclaimed as the world's worst poet.

Beautiful Railway Bridge of the Silv'ry Tay!
Alas! I am very sorry to say
That ninety lives have been taken away
On the last Sabbath day of 1879,
Which will be remember'd for a very long time.

'Twas about seven o'clock at night,
And the wind it blew with all its might,
And the rain came pouring down,
And the dark clouds seem'd to frown,
And the Demon of the air seem'd to say-
'I'll blow down the Bridge of Tay.'

When the train left Edinburgh
The passengers' hearts were light and felt no sorrow,
But Boreas blew a terrific gale,
Which made their hearts for to quail,
And many of the passengers with fear did say-
'I hope God will send us safe across the Bridge of Tay.'

But when the train came near to Wormit Bay,
Boreas he did loud and angry bray,
And shook the central girders of the Bridge of Tay
On the last Sabbath day of 1879,
Which will be remember'd for a very long time.

So the train sped on with all its might,
And Bonnie Dundee soon hove in sight,
And the passengers' hearts felt light,

Thinking they would enjoy themselves on the New Year,
With their friends at home they lov'd most dear,
And wish them all a happy New Year.

So the train mov'd slowly along the Bridge of Tay,
Until it was about midway,
Then the central girders with a crash gave way,
And down went the train and passengers into the Tay!
The Storm Fiend did loudly bray,
Because ninety lives had been taken away,
On the last Sabbath day of 1879,
Which will be remember'd for a very long time.

As soon as the catastrophe came to be known
The alarm from mouth to mouth was blown,
And the cry rang out all o'er the town,
Good Heavens! the Tay Bridge is blown down,
And a passenger train from Edinburgh,
Which fill'd all the peoples hearts with sorrow,
And made them for to turn pale,
Because none of the passengers were sav'd to tell the tale
How the disaster happen'd on the last Sabbath day of 1879,
Which will be remember'd for a very long time.

It must have been an awful sight,
To witness in the dusky moonlight,
While the Storm Fiend did laugh, and angry did bray,
Along the Railway Bridge of the Silv'ry Tay,
Oh! ill-fated Bridge of the Silv'ry Tay,
I must now conclude my lay
By telling the world fearlessly without the least dismay,
That your central girders would not have given way,
At least many sensible men do say,
Had they been supported on each side with buttresses,
At least many sensible men confesses,
For the stronger we our houses do build,
The less chance we have of being killed.

(From *Poetic Gems*; 1890)

The world's first public steam railway was George Stephenson's *Locomotion*

St Enoch Station, c1880

Eric Lomax

Lomax's story of his time in a Japanese prisoner of war camp working on the Burma-Siam Railway – a story of torture and subsequent reconciliation – was made into a moving film in 2013.

I have a painting in the hallway of my house in Berwick-upon-Tweed, by the Scottish artist Duncan Mackellar. It is a large work set in St Enoch Station in Glasgow on a dusty summer evening in the 1880s. A woman in late middle age, dressed in dark and modest clothes and carrying a parasol, is standing tense and distraught, looking out beyond us, oblivious of any other presence. Behind her the high smoke-grimed glass and wrought-iron walls of the station rise up. She is gazing off the edge of the platform at a vanishing train, so that we see her through the eyes of a receding traveller, and she has the flat restrained face of a person who has learned to swallow grief. Her sudden loneliness is captured as she strains to keep an image of her child, or so we assume, who is on the train heading for the emigrant ship or a colonial war - India, Afghanistan, the Gold Coast.

Although it is a conventional image, it is genuinely moving. I have always loved it. Railway stations have always attracted me, not just because trains are there, but because they are also ambivalent places, echoing with completed journeys and shrill with the melancholy noises of departure. Mackellar's painting is about the inevitability of separation, the cost of journeying. And we have never created any sound so evocative of separation as the whistle of a steam locomotive, that high note of inhuman relief as vaporized water is blown off and meets the cold air.

Once in the 1970s I went to St Enoch and stood on the platform at the spot that Mackellar's painting creates for the viewer, and the back of the great shed, like an enormous Victorian conservatory, seemed hardly to have changed. The station was not yet quite disused and silent, though a few years later it was destroyed, like so many of the other steam cathedrals. That age is gone now, finally, but the reality of grief, and the consequences of

the Stockton and Darlington Railway.
pulled the first carriages in 1825.

grief, of which Mackellar caught something in his painting, are not so easily banished.

The passion for trains and railways is, I have been told, incurable. I have also learned that there is no cure for torture. These two afflictions have been intimately linked in the course of my life, and yet through some chance combination of luck and grace I have survived them both. But it took me nearly fifty years to surmount the consequences of torture.

(From *The Railway Man*; Vintage, 1996, © Eric Lomax)

The Tunnel, 1881

THOMAS HARDY

Paula Power has inherited a castle which once belonged to the De Stancy family and employs a London architect, George Somerset, to help with its modernisation. She is torn between the feelings she has for a local man, William Dare who is descended from the De Stancys, and for Somerset (who stands for modernity and progress in the novel). They meet beside a tunnel on the newly-opened railway.

Somerset did not forget what he had planned, and when lunch was over he walked away through the trees. The tunnel was more difficult of discovery than he had anticipated, and it was only after considerable winding among green lanes, whose deep ruts were like canyons of Colorado in miniature, that he reached the slope in the distant upland where the tunnel began. A road stretched over its crest, and thence along one side of the railway-cutting.

He there unexpectedly saw standing Miss Power's carriage; and on drawing nearer he found it to contain Paula herself, Miss De Stancy, and Mrs. Goodman.

'How singular!' exclaimed Miss De Stancy gaily.

'It is most natural,' said Paula instantly. 'In the morning two people discuss a feature in the landscape, and in the afternoon each has a desire to see it from what the other has said of it. Therefore they accidentally meet.'

She had a penetrating sort of laugh. Rather like

Now Paula had distinctly heard Somerset declare that he was going to walk there; how then could she say this so coolly? It was with a pang at his heart that he returned to his old thought of her being possibly a finished coquette and dissembler. Whatever she might be, she was not a creature starched very stiffly by Puritanism.

Somerset looked down on the mouth of the tunnel. The popular commonplace that science, steam, and travel must always be unromantic and hideous, was not proven at this spot. On either slope of the deep cutting, green with long grass, grew drooping young trees of ash, beech, and other flexible varieties, their foliage almost concealing the actual railway which ran along the bottom, its thin steel rails gleaming like silver threads in the depths. The vertical front of the tunnel, faced with brick that had once been red, was now weather-stained, lichened, and mossed over in harmonious rusty-browns, pearly greys, and neutral greens, at the very base appearing a little blue-black spot like a mouse-hole – the tunnel's mouth.

The carriage was drawn up quite close to the wood railing, and Paula was looking down at the same time with him; but he made no remark to her.

Mrs. Goodman broke the silence by saying, 'If it were not a railway we should call it a lovely dell.'

Somerset agreed with her, adding that it was so charming that he felt inclined to go down.

'If you do, perhaps Miss Power will order you up again, as a trespasser,' said Charlotte De Stancy. 'You are one of the largest shareholders in the railway, are you not, Paula?'

Miss Power did not reply.

'I suppose as the road is partly yours you might walk all the way to London along the rails, if you wished, might you not, dear?' Charlotte continued.

Paula smiled, and said, 'No, of course not.'

Somerset, feeling himself superfluous, raised his hat to his

a train going into a tunnel. PG Wodehouse

companions as if he meant not to see them again for a while, and began to descend by some steps cut in the earth; Miss De Stancy asked Mrs. Goodman to accompany her to a barrow over the top of the tunnel; and they left the carriage, Paula remaining alone.

Down Somerset plunged through the long grass, bushes, late summer flowers, moths, and caterpillars, vexed with himself that he had come there, since Paula was so inscrutable, and humming the notes of some song he did not know. The tunnel that had seemed so small from the surface was a vast archway when he reached its mouth, which emitted, as a contrast to the sultry heat on the slopes of the cutting, a cool breeze, that had travelled a mile underground from the other end. Far away in the darkness of this silent subterranean corridor he could see that other end as a mere speck of light.

When he had conscientiously admired the construction of the massive archivault, and the majesty of its nude ungarnished walls, he looked up the slope at the carriage; it was so small to the eye that it might have been made for a performance by canaries; Paula's face being still smaller, as she leaned back in her seat, idly looking down at him. There seemed something roguish in her attitude of criticism, and to be no longer the subject of her contemplation he entered the tunnel out of her sight.

In the middle of the speck of light before him appeared a speck of black; and then a shrill whistle, dulled by millions of tons of earth, reached his ears from thence. It was what he had been on his guard against all the time – a passing train; and instead of taking the trouble to come out of the tunnel he stepped into a recess, till the train had rattled past and vanished onward round a curve.

Somerset still remained where he had placed himself, mentally balancing science against art, the grandeur of this fine piece of construction against that of the castle, and thinking whether Paula's father had not, after all, the best of it, when all at once he saw Paula's form confronting him at the entrance of the tunnel. He instantly went forward into the light; to his surprise she was as pale as a lily.

The distance is nothing when one has a motive.

'O, Mr. Somerset!' she exclaimed. 'You ought not to frighten me so – indeed you ought not! The train came out almost as soon as you had gone in, and as you did not return – an accident was possible!'

Somerset at once perceived that he had been to blame in not thinking of this.

'Please do forgive my thoughtlessness in not reflecting how it would strike you!' he pleaded. 'I – I see I have alarmed you.'

Her alarm was, indeed, much greater than he had at first thought: she trembled so much that she was obliged to sit down, at which he went up to her full of solicitousness.

'You ought not to have done it!' she said. 'I naturally thought – any person would – '

Somerset, perhaps wisely, said nothing at this outburst; the cause of her vexation was, plainly enough, his perception of her discomposure. He stood looking in another direction, till in a few moments she had risen to her feet again, quite calm.

'It would have been dreadful,' she said with faint gaiety, as the colour returned to her face; 'if I had lost my architect, and been obliged to engage Mr. Havill without an alternative.'

'I was really in no danger; but of course I ought to have considered,' he said.

'I forgive you,' she returned good-naturedly. 'I knew there was no GREAT danger to a person exercising ordinary discretion; but artists and thinkers like you are indiscreet for a moment sometimes. I am now going up again. What do you think of the tunnel?'

They were crossing the railway to ascend by the opposite path, Somerset keeping his eye on the interior of the tunnel for safety, when suddenly there arose a noise and shriek from the contrary direction behind the trees. Both knew in a moment what it meant, and each seized the other as they rushed off the permanent way. The ideas of both had been so centred on the tunnel as the source of danger, that the probability of a train from the opposite quarter had been forgotten. It rushed past them, causing Paula's dress, hair, and ribbons to flutter violently, and blowing up the fallen leaves in a shower over their shoulders.

Neither spoke, and they went up several steps, holding each other by the hand, till, becoming conscious of the fact, she withdrew hers; whereupon Somerset stopped and looked earnestly at her; but her eyes were averted towards the tunnel wall.

'What an escape!' he said.

'We were not so very near, I think, were we?' she asked quickly. 'If we were, I think you were – very good to take my hand.'

(From *A Laodicean: A Story of To-day, XII*; 1881)

From a Railway Carriage, 1885

Robert Louis Stevenson

Faster than fairies, faster than witches,
Bridges and houses, hedges and ditches;
And charging along like troops in a battle,
All through the meadows the houses and cattle;
All of the sights of the hill and the plain
Fly as thick as driving rain;
And ever again, in the wink of an eye,
Painted stations whistle by.

Here is a child who clambers and scrambles,
All by himself and gathering brambles;
Here is a tramp who stands and gazes;
And here is the green for stringing the daisies!
Here is a cart run away in the road
Lumping along with man and load;
And here is a mill and there is a river;
Each a glimpse and gone for ever!

(From *A Child's Garden of Verses*; 1885)

I love trains. I don't even mind First Great Western, which is but they're not.

Great Britain's Railways, 1890

KARL BAEDEKER

With his typical German precision, Baedeker describes the railways in Britain in great detail.

In proportion to area and population, the railway system of Great Britain is more extensive than that in any country in Europe, Belgium excepted. The length of lines in operation amounts to fully 17,000 miles, of which 14,000 are in England and Wales, and 3000 in Scotland. The lines are all in private hands, by far the greater part of the traffic being monopolised by ten or twelve large railway companies. These companies are Great Western with 2477 miles, London & North Western, with 1875½ miles, Midland with 1800 miles, North Eastern with 1578 miles, Great Eastern with 1112 miles, Great Northern with 936 miles, London & South Western with 815 miles, Lincolnshire & Yorkshire with 524 miles, London, Brighton & South Coast with 476 miles, South Eastern with 392½ miles, Manchester, Sheffield & Lincolnshire and Yorkshire with 290 miles, and London, Chatham and Dover with 194 miles.

The carriages (1st, 2nd, and 3rd class) of the more important companies are generally clean and comfortable, but those with some of the lines to the S. of London, as well as of most of the minor railways still surviving throughout the country, leave much to be desired.

To any would-be traveller who had any difficulties in understanding timetables, this range of choices of both line and company must have been a nightmare! However, at least some of the rules governing passengers had some similarity between companies. For example:

Each company is bound by Act of Parliament to run at least one train daily (known as the 'parliamentary train') at a fare in the 3rd class of not more than a penny a mile. However, the third class fares in many of these trains are considerably in excess of this rate. Return tickets are usually granted on very liberal terms; and circular tour tickets are issued in all the districts chiefly fre-

a stupid name because it implies every carriage is first class,
TIM RICE

quented by tourists. Smoking is not permitted except in the compartments provided for the purpose.

The speed of British trains is usually much higher than that of Continental Railways, and a rate of 40 to 50 miles an hour is not uncommon.

On all the English lines the first-class passenger is entitled to carry 112 lbs of luggage, second class 80 pounds and third class 60 pounds.

Travellers accustomed to the formality of Continental railways officials may perhaps consider they are much left to themselves. Tickets are not invariably checked at the beginning of a journey, and travellers should therefore make sure they are in the proper compartment. The names of the stations are not always so conspicuous as they should be, so the traveller needs to take care he knows where the train is stopping. ... The railway officials, however, are generally civil in answering questions and giving information. In winter, foot-warmers with hot water are usually provided. It is 'good form' for a passenger quitting a railway carriage where there are other travellers to close the door behind him, and to pull up the window if he has had to let it down to reach the door handle.

(From *Great Britain: Handbook for Travellers*; Karl Baedeker, 1890)

Thomas Cook, 1808-92

Obituary

Mr. Thomas Cook, the originator of the excursion system of railway travelling, and founder of the well-known firm of Messrs. Thomas Cook and Son, died at his residence, Thorncroft, Stonegate, Leicester, about midnight on Monday.

Born on November 22, 1808, at Melbourne, in Derbyshire, of very humble parentage, he had in his early years a severe struggle for the bare means of existence. He was only four years old when his father died, and he commenced to earn his daily bread at the age of ten, when he was employed in a village garden at the wage of 1d. a day. At this early age he contrived also to be of

I'm not in the top ten per cent of train spotters in Britain, but I do like trains.

material assistance to his mother, who kept a small shop for the sale of books. Soon afterwards he took to hawking fruit and vegetables in Derby market place, and a little later went to learn wood-turning. Afterwards he went to Loughborough, where he entered the employment of Mr. John Winks, a printer and publisher of books in connection with the General Baptist Association. In 1828 he was appointed a Bible reader and village missionary for the county of Rutland, and in the following year he travelled 2,692 miles, of which 2,106 miles were covered on foot.

Having in 1832 married Miss Mason, daughter of a Rutland farmer, he removed to Market Harborough, where, in addition to his work in connection with the Baptist Association, he carried on the business of a wood turner. In 1836 he became a total abstainer, and he was an ardent temperance reformer for the remainder of his life.

In 1841, while walking from Market Harborough to Leicester to attend a temperance meeting, he read in a newspaper a report of the opening of a part of the Midland Counties Railway, and the idea burst upon him that the new means of travel might be used for the benefit of the temperance movement. If, thought Mr. Cook, the railway company could be induced to run a special train from Leicester, many persons might be removed from the temptations of the races and great results might be achieved. He broached the subject to his friends, and arranged with the railway company for a special train to Loughborough on July 5, 1841. This, as we have on previous occasions pointed out, the first publicly advertised excursion train, conveyed no fewer than 570 passengers at 1s. each. The event caused great excitement. The passengers were preceded to the Leicester Station by a band of music. At Loughborough they were met by a great crowd of people, and they were welcomed home with equal enthusiasm.

The success of this trip induced Mr. Cook to combine the management of excursions with his book and printing business in Leicester, to which town he had removed. He organised trips to Derby, Nottingham, and Birmingham, and the business having grown so much that in several trips he conveyed between 4,000

and I don't know all about class numbers and such like,
MICHAEL PORTILLO

and 5,000 people, he in 1844 entered into permanent arrangements with the directors of the Midland Railway to place trains at his disposal whenever they were required while he provided the passengers. Next year saw an extension of the system to Liverpool, the Isle of Man, and Dublin. He also about this period organised a trip to Scotland, and conveyed 350 passengers from Leicester and Nottingham to Glasgow, where the excursionists received a warm welcome. His next move was to provide hotel coupons for his patrons, and Scotland was the field of his first endeavours in this direction. Personally conducted tours to Ireland followed, and in 1851 Mr. Cook conveyed many thousands of people to the Great Exhibition in Hyde Park.

The business began to extend in all directions in England and on the Continent. Mr. Cook's ambition was the institution of an annual tour round the world, which he successfully accomplished. His first tour round the world was in 1872, when he, with nine companions, started to make what he termed an exploratory tour. The tour was completed in 222 days. Mr. Cook retired from the firm in 1878, the business being then placed under the sole control of his son, Mr. John M. Cook.

(From *Railway News*; 23rd July 1892)

The Lost Special, 1898

Arthur Conan Doyle

The confession of Herbert de Lernac, now lying under sentence of death at Marseilles, has thrown a light upon one of the most inexplicable crimes of the century – an incident which is, I believe, absolutely unprecedented in the criminal annals of any country. Although there is a reluctance to discuss the matter in official circles, and little information has been given to the Press, there are still indications that the statement of this arch-criminal is corroborated by the facts, and that we have at last found a solution for a most astounding business. As the matter is eight years old, and as its importance was somewhat obscured by a political crisis which was engaging the public attention at the time, it may be as well to state the facts as far as we have been able to ascertain them. They are collated from the Liverpool papers of that date, from the proceedings at the inquest upon John Slater, the engine-driver, and from the records of the London and West Coast Railway Company, which have been courteously put at my disposal. Briefly, they are as follows:

On the 3rd of June, 1890, a gentleman, who gave his name as Monsieur Louis Caratal, desired an interview with Mr. James Bland, the superintendent of the London and West Coast Central Station in Liverpool. He was a small man, middle-aged and dark, with a stoop which was so marked that it suggested some deformity of the spine. He was accompanied by a friend, a man of imposing physique, whose deferential manner and constant attention showed that his position was one of dependence. This friend or companion, whose name did not transpire, was certainly a foreigner, and probably from his swarthy complexion, either a Spaniard or a South American. One peculiarity was observed in him. He carried in his left hand a small black, leather dispatch box, and it was noticed by a sharp-eyed clerk in the Central office that this box was fastened to his wrist by a strap. No importance was attached to the fact at the time, but subsequent events endowed it with some significance. Monsieur Caratal was shown up to Mr. Bland's office, while his companion remained outside.

☆ 2 ☆

Monsieur Caratal's business was quickly dispatched. He had arrived that afternoon from Central America. Affairs of the utmost importance demanded that he should be in Paris without the loss of an unnecessary hour. He had missed the London express. A special must be provided. Money was of no importance. Time was everything. If the company would speed him on his way, they might make their own terms.

Mr. Bland struck the electric bell, summoned Mr. Potter Hood, the traffic manager, and had the matter arranged in five minutes. The train would start in three-quarters of an hour. It would take that time to insure that the line should be clear. The powerful engine called Rochdale (No. 247 on the company's register) was attached to two carriages, with a guard's van behind. The first carriage was solely for the purpose of decreasing the

not both, and the same seems to apply to Great Train Robbers. Clive Anderson

inconvenience arising from the oscillation. The second was divided, as usual, into four compartments, a first-class, a first-class smoking, a second-class, and a second-class smoking. The first compartment, which was nearest to the engine, was the one allotted to the travellers. The other three were empty. The guard of the special train was James McPherson, who had been some years in the service of the company. The stoker, William Smith, was a new hand.

Monsieur Caratal, upon leaving the superintendent's office, rejoined his companion, and both of them manifested extreme impatience to be off. Having paid the money asked, which amounted to fifty pounds five shillings, at the usual special rate of five shillings a mile, they demanded to be shown the carriage, and at once took their seats in it, although they were assured that the better part of an hour must elapse before the line could be cleared. In the meantime a singular coincidence had occurred in the office which Monsieur Caratal had just quitted.

A request for a special is not a very uncommon circumstance in a rich commercial centre, but that two should be required upon the same afternoon was most unusual. It so happened, however, that Mr. Bland had hardly dismissed the first traveller before a second entered with a similar request. This was a Mr. Horace Moore, a gentlemanly man of military appearance, who alleged that the sudden serious illness of his wife in London made it absolutely imperative that he should not lose an instant in starting upon the journey. His distress and anxiety were so evident that Mr. Bland did all that was possible to meet his wishes. A second special was out of the question, as the ordinary local service was already somewhat deranged by the first. There was the alternative, however, that Mr. Moore should share the expense of Monsieur Caratal's train, and should travel in the other empty first-class compartment, if Monsieur Caratal objected to having him in the one which he occupied. It was difficult to see any objection to such an arrangement, and yet Monsieur Caratal, upon the suggestion being made to him by Mr. Potter Hood, absolutely refused to consider it for an instant. The train was his, he said, and he would insist upon the exclusive use of it. All argument failed to overcome his ungracious objections, and finally the plan had to be abandoned. Mr. Horace Moore left the station in great distress, after learning that his only course was to take the ordinary slow train which leaves Liverpool at six o'clock. At four thirty-one exactly by the station clock the special train, containing the crippled Monsieur Caratal and his gigantic companion, steamed out of the Liverpool station. The line was at that time clear, and there should have been no stoppage before Manchester.

☆ 3 ☆

The trains of the London and West Coast Railway run over the lines of another company as far as this town, which should have been reached by the special rather before six o'clock. At a quarter after six considerable surprise and some consternation were caused amongst the officials at Liverpool by the receipt of a telegram from Manchester to say that it had not yet arrived. An inquiry directed to St. Helens, which is a third of the way between the two cities, elicited the following reply -

'To James Bland, Superintendent, Central L. & W. C., Liverpool. – Special passed here at 4:52, well up to time. – Dowster, St. Helens.'

This telegram was received at six-forty. At six-fifty a second message was received from Manchester -

'No sign of special as advised by you.'

And then ten minutes later a third, more bewildering -

'Presume some mistake as to proposed running of special. Local train from St. Helens timed to follow it has just arrived and has seen nothing of it. Kindly wire advices. – Manchester.'

The matter was assuming a most amazing aspect, although in some respects the last telegram was a relief to the authorities at Liverpool. If an accident had occurred to the special, it seemed hardly possible that the local train could have passed down the same line without observing it. And yet, what was the alternative? Where could the train be? Had it possibly been sidetracked for some reason in order to allow the slower train to go past? Such an explanation was possible if some small repair had to be effected. A telegram was dispatched to each of the stations between St. Helens and Manchester, and the superintendent and traffic manager waited in the utmost suspense at the instrument for the series of replies which would enable them to say for certain what had become of the missing train. The answers came back in the order of questions, which was the order of the stations beginning at the St. Helens end -

☆ 4 ☆

'Special passed here five o'clock. – Collins Green.'

'Special passed here six past five. – Earlstown.'

'Special passed here 5:10. – Newton.'

'Special passed here 5:20. – Kenyon Junction.'

'No special train has passed here. – Barton Moss.'

The two officials stared at each other in amazement.

'This is unique in my thirty years of experience,' said Mr. Bland.

'Absolutely unprecedented and inexplicable, sir. The special has gone wrong between Kenyon Junction and Barton Moss.'

'And yet there is no siding, so far as my memory serves me, between the two stations. The special must have run off the metals.'

'But how could the four-fifty parliamentary pass over the same line without observing it?'

'There's no alternative, Mr. Hood. It must be so. Possibly the local train may have observed something which may throw some light upon the matter. We will wire to Manchester for more information, and to Kenyon Junction with instructions that the line be examined instantly as far as Barton Moss.' The answer from Manchester came within a few minutes.

'No news of missing special. Driver and guard of slow train positive no accident between Kenyon Junction and Barton Moss. Line quite clear, and no sign of anything unusual. – Manchester.'

'That driver and guard will have to go,' said Mr. Bland, grimly. 'There has been a wreck and they have missed it. The special has obviously run off the metals without disturbing the line – how it could have done so passes my comprehension – but so it must be, and we shall have a wire from Kenyon or Barton Moss presently to say that they have found her at the bottom of an embankment.'

☆ 5 ☆

But Mr. Bland's prophecy was not destined to be fulfilled. Half an hour passed, and then there arrived the following message from the station-master of Kenyon Junction -

'There are no traces of the missing special...'

For the continuation of this story see
http://www.eastoftheweb.com/short-stories/UBooks/LosSpe.shtml

(From *Tales of Terror and Mystery*; 1923)

The Railway Junction, 1902

Walter de la Mare

From here through tunnelled gloom the track
Forks into two; and one of these
Wheels onward into darkening hills,
And one toward distant seas.

How still it is; the signal light
At set of sun shines palely green;
A thrush sings; other sound there's none,
Nor traveller to be seen –

Where late there was a throng. And now,
In peace awhile, I sit alone;
Though soon, at the appointed hour,
I shall myself be gone.

But not their way (the bow-legged groom,
The parson in black, the widow and son,
The sailor with his cage, the gaunt
Gamekeeper with his gun.

That fair one too, discreetly veiled)
All, who so mutely came, and went,

because I knew somebody who could drive a diesel train.
Ronald Biggs

Will reach those far nocturnal hills
Or shores, ere night is spent.

I nothing know why thus we met –
Their thoughts, their longings, hopes, their fate:
And what shall I remember, except –
The evening growing late –

That here through tunnelled gloom the track
Forks into two; of these
One into darkening hills leads on,
And one toward distant seas?

(© From *Songs of Childhood* (under pen name Walter Ramal); Longman, 1902, © Walter de la Mare)

A Dragon in the Tunnel, 1906

E NESBIT

After realising that one of the grammar school boys on the paperchase has gone into the railway tunnel but not emerged at the other end, the three Railway Children decide they must go in themselves to find him despite being aware that it's 'against the bye-laws'.

Of course you know what going into a tunnel is like? The engine gives a scream and then suddenly the noise of the running, rattling train changes and grows different and much louder. Grown-up people pull up the windows and hold them by the strap. The railway carriage suddenly grows like night – with lamps, of course, unless you are in a slow local train, in which case lamps are not always provided. Then by and by the darkness outside the carriage window is touched by puffs of cloudy whiteness, then you see a blue light on the walls of the tunnel, then the sound of the moving train changes once more, and you are out in the good open air again, and grown-ups let the straps go. The windows, all dim with the yellow breath of the tunnel, rattle down into their places, and you see once more the dip and catch of the telegraph wires beside the line, and the straight-cut

The corsets I wore in *The Railway Children* are still in

hawthorn hedges with the tiny baby trees growing up out of them every thirty yards.

All this, of course, is what a tunnel means when you are in a train. But everything is quite different when you walk into a tunnel on your own feet, and tread on shifting, sliding stones and gravel on a path that curves downwards from the shining metals to the wall. Then you see slimy, oozy trickles of water running down the inside of the tunnel, and you notice that the bricks are not red or brown, as they are at the tunnel's mouth, but dull, sticky, sickly green. Your voice, when you speak, is quite changed from what it was out in the sunshine, and it is a long time before the tunnel is quite dark.

It was not yet quite dark in the tunnel when Phyllis caught at Bobbie's skirt, ripping out half a yard of gathers, but no one noticed this at the time.

'I want to go back,' she said, 'I don't like it. It'll be pitch dark in a minute. I WON'T go on in the dark. I don't care what you say, I WON'T.'

'Don't be a silly cuckoo,' said Peter; 'I've got a candle end and matches, and – what's that?'

'That' was a low, humming sound on the railway line, a trembling of the wires beside it, a buzzing, humming sound that grew louder and louder as they listened.

'It's a train,' said Bobbie.

'Which line?'

'Let me go back,' cried Phyllis, struggling to get away from the hand by which Bobbie held her.

'Don't be a coward,' said Bobbie; 'it's quite safe. Stand back.'

'Come on,' shouted Peter, who was a few yards ahead. 'Quick! Manhole!'

The roar of the advancing train was now louder than the noise you hear when your head is under water in the bath and both taps are running, and you are kicking with your heels against the bath's tin sides. But Peter had shouted for all he was

my undies drawer, a prized relic of my favourite film.
Dinah Sheridan

worth, and Bobbie heard him. She dragged Phyllis along to the manhole. Phyllis, of course, stumbled over the wires and grazed both her legs. But they dragged her in, and all three stood in the dark, damp, arched recess while the train roared louder and louder. It seemed as if it would deafen them. And, in the distance, they could see its eyes of fire growing bigger and brighter every instant.

'It IS a dragon – I always knew it was – it takes its own shape in here, in the dark,' shouted Phyllis. But nobody heard her. You see the train was shouting, too, and its voice was bigger than hers.

And now, with a rush and a roar and a rattle and a long dazzling flash of lighted carriage windows, a smell of smoke, and blast of hot air, the train hurtled by, clanging and jangling and echoing in the vaulted roof of the tunnel. Phyllis and Bobbie clung to each other. Even Peter caught hold of Bobbie's arm, 'in case she should be frightened,' as he explained afterwards.

And now, slowly and gradually, the tail-lights grew smaller and smaller, and so did the noise, till with one last WHIZ the train got itself out of the tunnel, and silence settled again on its damp walls and dripping roof.

'OH!' said the children, all together in a whisper.

(© From *The Railway Children*; Wells, Gardner, Darton, 1906)

Toad's Ticketless Travels, 1908

Kenneth Grahame

Here Toad boards a train … He was trying to return home after one of his misadventures. Disguised as a woman, he tries to hitch a lift on a railway engine, but – being Toad – that led to another adventure … though he had no money to pay his fare.

In his misery he made one desperate effort to carry the thing off, and, with a return to his fine old manner – a blend of the Squire and the College Don – he said, 'Look here! I find I've left my

I've travelled around the UK a lot recently and have nobody can get hold of you and

purse behind. Just give me that ticket, will you, and I'll send the money on tomorrow. I'm well known in these parts.'

The clerk stared at him and the rusty black bonnet a moment, and then laughed. 'I should think you were pretty well known in these parts,' he said, 'if you've tried this game on often. Here, stand away from the window, please, madam; you're obstructing the other passengers!'

Baffled and full of despair, he wandered blindly down the platform where the train was standing, and tears trickled down each side of his nose. It was hard, he thought, to be within sight of safety and almost of home, and to be baulked by the want of a few wretched shillings and by the pettifogging mistrustfulness of paid officials. Very soon his escape (from prison) would be discovered, the hunt would be up, he would be caught, reviled, loaded with chains, dragged back again to prison, and bread-and-water and straw; his guards and penalties would be doubled; and O what sarcastic remarks the girls would make!

What was to be done?

He was not swift of foot; his figure was unfortunately recognizable. Could he not squeeze under the seat of a carriage? He had seen this method adopted by schoolboys, when the journey money provided by thoughtful parents had been diverted to other and better ends. As he pondered he found himself opposite the engine, which was being oiled, wiped, and generally caressed by its affectionate driver. A burly man with an oil can in one hand a lump of cotton waste in the other.

'Hullo, mother!' said the engine driver, 'what's the trouble? You don't look particularly cheerful.'

'O, sir,!' said Toad, crying afresh, 'I am a poor unhappy washerwoman, and I've lost all my money, and can't pay for a ticket, and I must get home tonight somehow, and whatever am I to do I don't know. O dear, O dear!'

Toad wove a story about his fictional children until the engine driver began to take pity on him … and eventually allowed Toad to scramble up into the engine … . The guard waved his welcome flag, the engineer driver whistled in cheerful response, and the train moved out of the station … .

discovered I really like trains. If you're in the quiet carriage, you can relax. HONOR BLACKMAN

They had covered many and many a mile, and Toad was already considering what he could have for supper as soon as he got home, when he noticed that the engine driver, with a puzzled expression on his face, was leaning over the side of the engine and listening hard. Then he saw him climb on the coals and gaze out over the top of the train; then he returned and said to Toad, 'It's very strange; we're the last train running in this direction tonight, yet I could have sworn that I heard another following us!'

(From *The Wind in the Willows*; Methuen, 1908)

Going to Work, 1910

ARNOLD BENNETT

In his popular self-help book, 'How to Live on Twenty-Four Hours a Day', Bennett showed his readers how to find extra time – such as when travelling on the train to work – which they could then make the most of by using it to improve themselves perhaps by reading great works of literature.

If my typical man wishes to live fully and completely he must, in his mind, arrange a day within a day. And this inner day, a Chinese box in a larger Chinese box, must begin at 6 p.m. and end at 10 a.m. It is a day of sixteen hours; and during all these sixteen hours he has nothing whatever to do but cultivate his body and his soul and his fellow men. During those sixteen hours he is free; he is not a wage-earner; he is not preoccupied with monetary cares; he is just as good as a man with a private income. This must be his attitude.

☆ ☆ ☆

I shall now examine the typical man's current method of employing the sixteen hours that are entirely his, beginning with his uprising. ..... In justice to him I must say that he wastes very little time before he leaves the house in the morning at 9.10. In too many houses he gets up at nine, breakfasts between 9.07 and 9.09 ½, and then bolts. But immediately he bangs the front door his mental faculties, which are tireless, become idle. He walks to the

Railway termini are our gates to the glorious and the sunshine; to them,

station in a condition of mental coma. Arrived there, he usually has to wait for the train. On hundreds of suburban stations every morning you see men calmly strolling up and down platforms while railway companies unblushingly rob them of time, which is more than money. Hundreds of thousands of hours are thus lost every day simply because my typical man thinks so little of time that it has never occurred to him to take quite easy precautions against the risk of its loss.

He has a solid coin of time to spend every day – call it a sovereign. He must get change for it, and in getting change he is content to lose heavily. Supposing that in selling him a ticket the company said, 'We will change you a sovereign, but we shall charge you three half-pence for doing so,' what would my typical man exclaim? Yet that is the equivalent of what the company does when it robs him of five minutes twice a day .... .

You say I am dealing with minutiae. I am. And later on I will justify myself. Now will you kindly buy your newspaper and step into the train?

(From *How to Live on Twenty-Four Hours a Day*; 1910)

Adlestrop, 1914

EDWARD THOMAS

This Cotswold village was immortalised in Edward Thomas's very poignant poem of the same name, written just before the start of the First World War. When the train stopped at Adlestrop he was on his way to meet the poet Robert Frost who helped him overcome his lack of confidence and encouraged him to write. Three years of brilliant creativity followed 'Adlestrop' but on 9th April 1917, on the first day of the Battle of Arras, he was killed in action.

Yes. I remember Adlestrop –
The name, because one afternoon
Of heat the express-train drew up there
Unwontedly. It was late June.

unknown. Through them we pass out into adventure and alas! we return. EM FORSTER

The steam hissed. Someone cleared his throat.
No one left and no one came
On the bare platform. What I saw
Was Adlestrop – only the name

And willows, willow-herb, and grass,
And meadowsweet, and haycocks dry,
No whit less still and lonely fair
Than the high cloudlets in the sky.

And for that minute a blackbird sang
Close by, and round him, mistier,
Farther and farther, all the birds
Of Oxfordshire and Gloucestershire.

(From *Collected Poems*; Faber & Faber, 1920)

On the Departure Platform, 1916

THOMAS HARDY

We kissed at the barrier; and passing through
She left me, and moment by moment got
Smaller and smaller, until to my view
    She was but a spot;

A wee white spot of muslin fluff
That down the diminishing platform bore
Through hustling crowds of gentle and rough
    To the carriage door.

Under the lamplight's fitful glowers,
Behind dark groups from far and near,
Whose interests were apart from ours,
    She would disappear,

Then show again, till I ceased to see
That flexible form, that nebulous white;

The highest railway in the UK is the Snowden Mountain

And she who was more than my life to me
Had vanished quite.

We have penned new plans since that fair fond day,
And in season she will appear again –
Perhaps in the same soft white array –
But never as then!

– 'And why, young man, must eternally fly
A joy you'll repeat, if you love her well ?'
– O friend, nought happens twice thus; why,
I cannot tell!

(From *Selected Poems of Thomas Hardy*; Macmillan, 1916)

Morning Express, 1918

Siegfried Sassoon

Along the wind-swept platform, pinched and white,
The travellers stand in pools of wintry light,
Offering themselves to morn's long slanting arrows.
The train's due; porters trundle laden barrows.
The train steams in, volleying resplendent clouds
Of sun-blown vapour. Hither and about,
Scared people hurry, storming the doors in crowds.
The officials seem to waken with a shout,
Resolved to hoist and plunder; some to the vans
Leap; others rumble the milk in gleaming cans.

Boys, indolent-eyed, from baskets leaning back,
Question each face; a man with a hammer steals
Stooping from coach to coach; with clang and clack,
Touches and tests, and listens to the wheels.
Guard sounds a warning whistle, points to the clock
With brandished flag, and on his folded flock
Claps the last door: the monster grunts; 'Enough!'
Tightening his load of links with pant and puff.

Railway which reaches 1064m (3490ft) on Mt Snowden.

Under the arch, then forth into blue day;
Glide the processional windows on their way,
And glimpse the stately folk who sit at ease
To view the world like kings taking the seas
In prosperous weather: drifting banners tell
Their progress to the counties; with them goes
The clamour of their journeying; while those
Who sped them stand to wave a last farewell.

(From *The Old Huntsman and Other Poems*; EP Dutton, 1918, © Siegfried Sassoon)

The Send-off, 1918

WILFRED OWEN

This is one of Wilfred Owen's most famous poems. Written at Ripon, it describes the departure of a troop train. Owen came back from the trenches in 1915, suffering from shell shock, and in hospital he met Siegfried Sassoon who helped him with both his trauma and his poetry. Awarded the Military Cross for bravery, he was killed in 1918, a week before the end of the war.

Down the close, darkening lanes they sang their way
To the siding-shed,
And lined the train with faces grimly gay.
Their breasts were stuck all white with wreath and spray
As men's are, dead.

Dull porters watched them, and a casual tramp
Stood staring hard,
Sorry to miss them from the upland camp.
Then, unmoved, signals nodded, and a lamp
Winked to the guard.

So secretly, like wrongs hushed-up, they went.
They were not ours:
We never heard to which front these were sent.

Humanity does not pass through phases as a train passes moving yet never leaving

Nor there if they yet mock what women meant
Who gave them flowers.

Shall they return to beatings of great bells
In wild trainloads?
A few, a few, too few for drums and yells,
May creep back, silent, to still village wells
Up half-known roads.

(From *Poems*; 1920)

Night Mail, 1936

WH Auden

This poem was written for the 1936 documentary, 'Night Mail', produced by the GPO film unit to show how post was sorted and distributed on this postal special train, which ran overnight between London and Aberdeen, via Glasgow and Edinburgh. With its soundtrack by Benjamin Britten, the film has become something of a classic.

This is the Night Mail crossing the border,
Bringing the cheque and the postal order,
Letters for the rich, letters for the poor,
The shop at the corner and the girl next door.
Pulling up Beattock, a steady climb:
The gradient's against her, but she's on time.
Past cotton-grass and moorland boulder
Shovelling white steam over her shoulder,
Snorting noisily as she passes
Silent miles of wind-bent grasses.

Birds turn their heads as she approaches,
Stare from the bushes at her blank-faced coaches.
Sheep-dogs cannot turn her course;
They slumber on with paws across.
In the farm she passes no one wakes,
But a jug in the bedroom gently shakes.

through stations: being alive, it has the privilege of always anything behind. CS Lewis

Dawn freshens, the climb is done.
Down towards Glasgow she descends
Towards the steam tugs yelping down the glade of cranes,
Towards the fields of apparatus, the furnaces
Set on the dark plain like gigantic chessmen.
All Scotland waits for her:
In the dark glens, beside the pale-green sea lochs
Men long for news.

Letters of thanks, letters from banks,
Letters of joy from the girl and the boy,
Receipted bills and invitations
To inspect new stock or to visit relations,
And applications for situations
And timid lovers' declarations
And gossip, gossip from all the nations,
News circumstantial, news financial,
Letters with holiday snaps to enlarge in,
Letters with faces scrawled on the margin,
Letters from uncles, cousins, and aunts,
Letters to Scotland from the South of France,
Letters of condolence to Highlands and Lowlands
Notes from overseas to the Hebrides
Written on paper of every hue,
The pink, the violet, the white and the blue,
The chatty, the catty, the boring, the adoring,
The cold and official and the heart's outpouring,
Clever, stupid, short and long,
The typed and the printed and the spelt all wrong.

Thousands are still asleep
Dreaming of terrifying monsters,
Or of friendly tea beside the band in Cranston's or Crawford's:
Asleep in working Glasgow, asleep in well-set Edinburgh,
Asleep in granite Aberdeen,
They continue their dreams,
And shall wake soon and hope for letters,

And none will hear the postman's knock
Without a quickening of the heart,
For who can bear to feel himself forgotten?

(From *Night Mail*; GPO Film Unit, 1936, © WH Auden)

Skimbleshanks: The Railway Cat, 1939

TS Eliot

Skimbleshanks was the cat that lived on the Night Mail, the train that ran each night between London and Scotland...

There's a whisper down the line at 11.39
When the Night Mail's ready to depart,
Saying 'Skimble where is Skimble has he gone to hunt the
thimble?
We must find him or the train can't start.'
All the guards and all the porters and the stationmaster's
daughters
They are searching high and low,
Saying 'Skimble where is Skimble for unless he's very nimble
Then the Night Mail just can't go.'
At 11.42 then the signal's nearly due
And the passengers are frantic to a man –
Then Skimble will appear and he'll saunter to the rear:
He's been busy in the luggage van!
He gives one flash of his glass-green eyes
And the signal goes 'All Clear!'
And we're off at last for the northern part
Of the Northern Hemisphere!

You may say that by and large it is Skimble who's in charge
Of the Sleeping Car Express.
From the driver and the guards to the bagmen playing cards
He will supervise them all, more or less.
Down the corridor he paces and examines all the faces
Of the travellers in the First and in the Third;

arrival, matters. TS Eliot

He establishes control by a regular patrol
And he'd know at once if anything occurred.
He will watch you without winking and he sees what you
  are thinking
And it's certain that he doesn't approve
Of hilarity and riot, so the folk are very quiet
When Skimble is about and on the move.
  You can play no pranks with Skimbleshanks!
  He's a Cat that cannot be ignored;
  So nothing goes wrong on the Northern Mail
  When Skimbleshanks is aboard.

Oh it's very pleasant when you have found your little den
With your name written up on the door.
And the berth is very neat with a newly folded sheet
And there's not a speck of dust on the floor.
There is every sort of light – you can make it dark or bright;
There's a button that you turn to make a breeze.
There's a funny little basin you're supposed to wash your face in
And a crank to shut the window if you sneeze.
Then the guard looks in politely and will ask you very brightly
'do you like your morning tea weak or strong?'
But Skimble's just behind him and was ready to remind him,
For Skimble won't let anything go wrong.
And when you creep into your cosy berth
And pull up the counterpane,
  You are bound to admit that it's very nice
  To know that you won't be bothered by mice –
  You can leave all that to the Railway Cat,
  The Cat of the Railway Train!

In the middle of the night he is always fresh and bright;
Every now and then he has a cup of tea
With perhaps a drop of Scotch while he's keeping on the watch,
Only stopping here and there to catch a flea.
You were fast asleep at Crewe and so you never knew
That he was walking up and down the station;

You were sleeping all the while he was busy at Carlisle,
Where he greets the stationmaster with elation.
But you saw him at Dumfries, where he summons the police
If there's anything they ought to know about:
when you get to Gallowgate there you do not have to wait –
For Skimbleshanks will help you to get out!
He gives you a wave of his long brown tail
Which says: 'I'll see you again!
You'll meet without fail on the Midnight Mail
The Cat of the Railway Train.'

(From *Old Possum's Book of Practical Cats*; Faber & Faber, 1939, © TS Eliot)

The Whitsun Weddings, 1958

Philip Larkin

In 2014 a plaque was unveiled at London's King's Cross station to mark the 50th anniversary of the original publication of the collection of Philip Larkin's finest poetry, this poem being the title piece. In it Larkin describes his journey from Yorkshire to London on a hot Whitsun weekend so vividly we feel as if we are in that carriage with him...

That Whitsun, I was late getting away:
Not till about
One-twenty on the sunlit Saturday
Did my three-quarters-empty train pull out,
All windows down, all cushions hot, all sense
Of being in a hurry gone. We ran
Behind the backs of houses, crossed a street
Of blinding windscreens, smelt the fish-dock; thence
The river's level drifting breadth began,
Where sky and Lincolnshire and water meet.

All afternoon, through the tall heat that slept
For miles inland,
A slow and stopping curve southwards we kept.
Wide farms went by, short-shadowed cattle, and

somewhere else. **Tom Stoppard**

Canals with floatings of industrial froth;
A hothouse flashed uniquely: hedges dipped
And rose: and now and then a smell of grass
Displaced the reek of buttoned carriage-cloth
Until the next town, new and nondescript,
Approached with acres of dismantled cars.

At first, I didn't notice what a noise
    The weddings made
Each station that we stopped at: sun destroys
The interest of what's happening in the shade,
And down the long cool platforms whoops and skirls
I took for porters larking with the mails,
And went on reading. Once we started, though,
We passed them, grinning and pomaded, girls
In parodies of fashion, heels and veils,
All posed irresolutely, watching us go,

As if out on the end of an event
    Waving goodbye
To something that survived it. Struck, I leant
More promptly out next time, more curiously,
And saw it all again in different terms:
The fathers with broad belts under their suits
And seamy foreheads; mothers loud and fat;
An uncle shouting smut; and then the perms,
The nylon gloves and jewellery-substitutes,
The lemons, mauves, and olive-ochres that

Marked off the girls unreally from the rest.
    Yes, from cafés
And banquet-halls up yards, and bunting-dressed
Coach-party annexes, the wedding-days
Were coming to an end. All down the line
Fresh couples climbed aboard: the rest stood round;
The last confetti and advice were thrown,
And, as we moved, each face seemed to define

Just what it saw departing: children frowned
At something dull; fathers had never known

Success so huge and wholly farcical;
The women shared
The secret like a happy funeral;
While girls, gripping their handbags tighter, stared
At a religious wounding. Free at last,
And loaded with the sum of all they saw,
We hurried towards London, shuffling gouts of steam.
Now fields were building-plots, and poplars cast
Long shadows over major roads, and for
Some fifty minutes, that in time would seem

Just long enough to settle hats and say
I nearly died,
A dozen marriages got under way.
They watched the landscape, sitting side by side
– An Odeon went past, a cooling tower,
And someone running up to bowl – and none
Thought of the others they would never meet
Or how their lives would all contain this hour.
I thought of London spread out in the sun,
Its postal districts packed like squares of wheat:

There we were aimed. And as we raced across
Bright knots of rail
Past standing Pullmans, walls of blackened moss
Came close, and it was nearly done, this frail
Travelling coincidence; and what it held
stood ready to be loosed with all the power
That being changed can give. We slowed again,
And as the tightened brakes took hold, there swelled
A sense of falling, like an arrow-shower
Sent out of sight, somewhere becoming rain.

(From *The Collected Poems;* Faber & Faber 1993, © Philip Larkin)

Slow Train, 1963

FLANDERS & SWANN

'No, I think I agree with the old lady who said, 'if God had intended us to fly, He would never have given us the railways!' So we've written a song about the railways instead. Unusual song this for us, perhaps, because it's really quite a serious song, and it was suggested by all those marvelous old local railway stations with their wonderful evocative names, all due to be, you know, axed and done away with one by one, and these are stations that we shall no longer be seeing when we aren't able to travel anymore on the slow train'.

Miller's Dale for Tideswell ...
Kirby Muxloe ...
Mow Cop and Scholar Green ...

No more will I go to Blandford Forum and Mortehoe
On the slow train from Midsomer Norton and Mumby Road.
No churns, no porter, no cat on a seat
At Chorlton-cum-Hardy or Chester-le-Street.
We won't be meeting again
On the Slow Train.

I'll travel no more from Littleton Badsey to Openshaw.
At Long Stanton I'll stand well clear of the doors no more.
No whitewashed pebbles, no Up and no Down
From Formby Four Crosses to Dunstable Town.
I won't be going again
On the Slow Train.

On the Main Line and the Goods Siding
The grass grows high
At Dog Dyke, Tumby Woodside
And Trouble House Halt.

The Sleepers sleep at Audlem and Ambergate.

**When I was at school I used to scream in trains,
I used to try to be so good that sometimes**

No passenger waits on Chittening platform or Cheslyn Hay.
No one departs, no one arrives
From Selby to Goole, from St Erth to St Ives.
They've all passed out of our lives
On the Slow Train, on the Slow Train.

Cockermouth for Buttermere ... on the Slow Train,
Armley Moor Arram ...
Pye Hill and Somercotes ... on the Slow Train,
Windmill End.

(From *At the Drop of Another Hat*; 1963, © Flanders & Swann)

Great Central Railway, Sheffield Victoria to Banbury, 1966

JOHN BETJEMAN

Sir John Betjeman was Poet Laureate from 1972 until his death in 1984. He was also a writer and broadcaster with a passion for Victorian architecture and an interest in railways. His poetry is often humorous, sometimes nostalgic and usually quite accessible

'Unmitigated England'
Came swinging down the line
That day the February sun
Did crisp and crystal shine.
Dark red at Kirkby Bentinck stood
A steeply gabled farm
'Mid ash trees and a sycamore
In charismatic calm.
A village street {---} a manor house {---}
A church {---} then, tally ho!
We pounded through a housing scheme
With tellymasts a-row,
Where cars of parked executives
Did regimented wait
Beside administrative blocks

in those concertina things between the carriages. I couldn't bear it any more. JANE BIRKIN

Within the factory gate.
She waved to us from Hucknall South
As we hooted round a bend,
From a curtained front-window did
The diesel driver's friend.
Through cuttings deep to Nottingham
Precariously we wound;
The swallowing tunnel made the train
Seem London's Underground.
Above the fields of Leicestershire
On arches we were borne.

And the rumble of the railway drowned
The thunder of the Quorn;
And silver shone the steeples out
Above the barren boughs;
Colts in a paddock ran from us
But not the solid cows;
And quite where Rugby Central is
Does only Rugby know.
We watched the empty platform wait
And sadly saw it go.
By now the sun of afternoon
Showed ridge and furrow shadows
And shallow unfamiliar lakes
Stood shivering in the meadows.
Is Woodford church or Hinton church
The one I ought to see?
Or were they both too much restored
In 1883?
I do not know. Towards the west
A trail of glory runs
And we leave the old Great Central line
For Banbury and buns.

(From *High and Low*; John Murray, 1966, © John Betjeman)

One of the gladdest moments of human life, methinks, is Shaking off ... the fetters of habit, the leaden weight

Reading the Nuances of Train Travel, 2007

Stuart Maconie

As a non-driver without a desk job, I spend my life on trains. I have become skilled in reading every nuance of train travel. I can tell by the timbre of the intercom's chime whether it's good or bad news. I know by the way the engine dies just how long we'll be in this siding in Nuneaton. I know instinctively when we're going to be diverted via Leighton Buzzard. I can play the network like one of those American railway hobos Bob Dylan wanted to be, knowing just where to change for Penrith on a Friday night, which carriage to sit in to make the quickest time from platform six into the new Bullring shopping centre in Birmingham, how much the Opal Fruits are on the trolley. I have become immune to and philosophical about some railway irritants and increasingly irritated by others. I'm currently obsessed with the way the 'senior conductor', drunk with power and the sound of his own voice crackling through the PA, will declaim with the verbiage and prolixity of Larry Olivier doing Shakespeare, until something goes wrong, when he suddenly turns into Buster Keaton doing Harold Pinter, all mysterious pauses and menacing silences. They lovingly list, as if this were the 12.20 from Frankfurt to Dusseldorf circa 1938, all the things you can't do, the tickets you can't travel with, the noises you can't make, the things you can't eat, the places you can't put your bag and so on before becoming oddly mute and uninformative when you actually need to know something useful, like why we've been stuck in a tunnel near High Wycombe for three hours.

(From *Pies and Prejudice*; Ebury Press, 2007, © Stuart Maconie)

Darsham Station in Suffolk, 2014

Deborah Manley

My parents used to live in East Suffolk and their local station was Darsham, where the level crossing of the road north meant that the gates had to be shut when a train was approaching along the railway line. There were usually only a few people using the train and there was talk of the line being closed. The community up and down the line was determined to keep it open. Had it closed they would have been dependent on their cars – if they had one and could drive – or the very infrequent buses, mostly going only from one village and small town to another.

There was a splendidly organised protest. People who usually used the train all joined in – and brought their usual 'luggage' with them: perhaps two toddlers in a pram, large artist's folders (for several artists lived in the area), a woman in a wheelchair, young people with a lot of luggage as they returned to college, and older people with slightly less, but still heavy, luggage. That was twenty years ago so we were very pleased to find the station still open last year when my son joined us from London one evening.

We stood in the circle of light in the dark night as cars rumbled past on the level crossing. Then bells sounded and lights flashed. The crossing gates swung together across the road. And, out of the dark, came the vast train, lit up so we could see the people gathering their belongings to descend or, if they were going further, looking out at us on the station platform. Soon my son was with us and the train started off again into the darkness. And all was silent again.

How grateful we were to those people who had fought to keep this railway line – and succeeded.

I dislike feeling at home when I am abroad.
GK CHESTERTON

CONTINENTAL EUROPE 2

The Calais Night Mail, 1851

CHARLES DICKENS

Calais up and doing at the railway station and Calais down and dreaming in its bed; Calais with something of an ancient and fish-like smell about it, and Calais blown and sea-washed pure; Calais represented at the buffet by savoury roast fowls, hot coffee, cognac and Bordeaux; and Calais represented everywhere by flitting persons with a monomania for changing money – although I shall never be able to understand in my present state of existence how they live by it, but I suppose I should if I understood the currency question, Calais *en gros* and Calais *en detail* forgive one who has deeply wronged you – I was not fully aware of it on the other side, but I meant Dover.

Ding! – ding! To the carriages, gentlemen the travellers. Ascend then gentlemen, the travellers for Hazebroucke, Lille, Douai, Bruxelles, Arras, Amiens and Paris. I, humble representative of the non-commercial interest, ascend with the rest. The train is light tonight and I share my compartment with but two fellow travellers: one a compatriot in an obsolete cravat, who thinks it is a quite unaccountable thing that they don't keep 'London time' on a French railway, and who is made angry by my modestly suggesting of Paris time being more in their way; the other, a young priest, with a very small bird in a very small cage, who feeds the small bird with a quill, and then puts him up on the network above his head, where he advances, twittering, to his front wires, and seems to address me in an electioneering manner. The compatriot, who crossed in the boat, and the young priest are soon asleep, and then the bird and I have it all to ourselves.

A stormy night still; a night that sweeps the wires of the electric telegraph with a wild and fitful hand; a night so very stormy, with the added storm of the train-progress through it, that when the Guard comes clambering round to mark the tickets while we are at full speed (a really horrible performance in an express train, though he holds on to the open window by his elbows in the most deliberate manner), he stands in such a whirlwind that I grip him fast by the collar, and feel it next to manslaughter to let him go. Still, when he is gone, the small, small bird remains at his front wires feebly twittering to me--twittering and twittering, until, leaning back in my place and looking at him in drowsy fascination, I find that he seems to jog my memory as we rush along.

(From *The Uncommercial Traveller*; 1860)

A Broken Vow, 1902

Hilaire Belloc

Hilaire Belloc had an illustrious life as Liberal politician, soldier, public speaker, satirist and poet. He is probably best known for his 'Cautionary Tales for Children'. He was a devout Catholic and in 1902 walked from central France to Rome, the account of which was published as 'The Path to Rome'. In this extract, Belloc seeks divine help in Como and is directed to take the train to Milan.

So I went on till I got to the lake, and there I found a little port about as big as a dining-room (for the Italian lakes play at being little seas. They have little ports, little lighthouses, little fleets for war, and little custom-houses, and little storms and little lines of steamers. Indeed, if one wanted to give a rich child a perfect model or toy, one could not give him anything better than an Italian lake), and when I had long gazed at the town, standing, as it seemed, right in the lake, I felt giddy, and said to myself, 'This is the lack of food,' for I had eaten nothing but my coffee and bread eleven miles before, at dawn.

So I pulled out my two francs, and going into a little shop, I bought bread, sausage, and a very little wine for fourpence, and

The lowest railway line in Europe is in the Channel

with one franc eighty left I stood in the street eating and wondering what my next step should be.

It seemed on the map perhaps twenty-five, perhaps twenty-six miles to Milan. It was now nearly noon, and as hot as could be. I might, if I held out, cover the distance in eight or nine hours, but I did not see myself walking in the middle heat on the plain of Lombardy, and even if I had been able I should only have got into Milan at dark or later, when the post office (with my money in it) would be shut; and where could I sleep, for my one franc eighty would be gone? A man covering these distances must have one good meal a day or he falls ill. I could beg, but there was the risk of being arrested, and that means an indefinite waste of time, perhaps several days; and time, that had defeated me at the Gries, threatened me here again. I had nothing to sell or to pawn, and I had no friends. The Consul I would not attempt; I knew too much of such things as Consuls when poor and dirty men try them. Besides which, there was no Consul I pondered.

I went into the cool of the cathedral to sit in its fine darkness and think better. I sat before a shrine where candles were burning, put up for their private intentions by the faithful. Of many, two had nearly burnt out. I watched them in their slow race for extinction when a thought took me.

'I will,' said I to myself, 'use these candles for an ordeal or heavenly judgement. The left hand one shall be for attempting the road at the risk of illness or very dangerous failure; the right hand one shall stand for my going by rail till I come to that point on the railway where one franc eighty will take me, and thence walking into Milan: – and heaven defend the right.'

They were a long time going out, and they fell evenly. At last the right hand one shot up the long flame that precedes the death of candles; the contest took on interest, and even excitement, when, just as I thought the left hand certain of winning, it went out without guess or warning, like a second-rate person leaving this world for another. The right hand candle waved its flame still higher, as though in triumph, outlived its colleague just the moment to enjoy glory, and then in its turn went fluttering down the dark way from which they say there is no return.

Tunnel, where the rails are 127m (416ft) below sea level.

None may protest against the voice of the Gods. I went straight to the nearest railway station (for there are two), and putting down one franc eighty, asked in French for a ticket to whatever station that sum would reach down the line. The ticket came out marked Milan, and I admitted the miracle and confessed the finger of Providence. There was no change, and as I got into the train I had become that rarest and ultimate kind of traveller, the man without any money whatsoever – without passport, without letters, without food or wine; it would be interesting to see what would follow if the train broke down.

I had marched 378 miles and some three furlongs, or thereabouts.

Thus did I break – but by a direct command – the last and dearest of my vows, and as the train rumbled off, I took luxury in the rolling wheels.

I thought of that other medieval and papistical pilgrim hobbling along rather than 'take advantage of any wheeled thing', and I laughed at him.

Now if Moroso-Malodoroso or any other Non-Aryan, Antichristian, over-inductive, statistical, brittle-minded man and scientist, sees anything remarkable in one self laughing at another self, let me tell him and all such for their wide-eyed edification and astonishment that I knew a man once that had fifty-six selves (there would have been fifty-seven, but for the poet in him that died young) – he could evolve them at will, and they were very useful to lend to the parish priest when he wished to make up a respectable Procession on Holy-days. And I knew another man that could make himself so tall as to look over the heads of the scientists as a pine-tree looks over grasses, and again so small as to discern very clearly the thick coating or dust of wicked pride that covers them up in a fine impenetrable coat. So much for the moderns.

The train rolled on. I noticed Lombardy out of the windows. It is flat. I listened to the talk of the crowded peasants in the train. I did not understand it. I twice leaned out to see if Milan were not standing up before me out of the plain, but I saw nothing. Then I fell asleep, and when I woke suddenly it was because we were in

The lowest railway line in the world is in the Seikan
the rails are 240m

the terminus of that noble great town, which I then set out to traverse in search of my necessary money and sustenance. It was yet but early in the afternoon.

What a magnificent city is Milan! The great houses are all of stone, and stand regular and in order, along wide straight streets. There are swift cars, drawn by electricity, for such as can afford them. Men are brisk and alert even in the summer heats, and there are shops of a very good kind, though a trifle showy. There are many newspapers to help the Milanese to be better men and to cultivate charity and humility; there are banks full of paper money; there are soldiers, good pavements, and all that man requires to fulfil him, soul and body; cafés, arcades, mutoscopes, and every sign of the perfect state. And the whole centres in a splendid open square, in the midst of which is the cathedral, which is justly the most renowned in the world.

(From *The Path to Rome*; Longmans, Green & Co, 1902, © Hilaire Belloc)

Around Mount Ætna, 1903

KARL BAEDEKER

Popular with foreign visitors, the narrow gauge railway line that almost circumnavigates this famous volcano in Sicily still operates today.

Ferrovia Circumetnea from Riposto to Catanai, 68M, in 5½-7½ hours.

This line, which traverses some interesting scenery, ascends to the upper limits of the cultivated zone, thus affording, even to those who do not visit the summit of Mount Ætna, an opportunity of noting the varied character of the mountain. Ætna is sometimes ascended from Randazzo, a station on this section of the line, and also from Biancavilla or Linguaglossa. The inns are, on the whole, poor. The Giarre station of the Ferrovia Circumetnea lies only 250 yds. to the west of that of the main railway, so that Giarre is the most convenient starting point. Those who use the morning train have the best chance of a clear view of Mount Ætna.

Tunnel between Honshu and Hokkaido in Japan, where (787ft) below sea level.

The line runs to the west, crosses the highroad and the Torrente Macchia, and then turns to the north, gradually ascending along the hillside and traversing the beds of several torrents.

At 3 miles is Cutula. To the left rise the outskirts of Mount Ætna; to the right, in the distance, are the rocky hills of Taormina. Beyond (5 miles) Santa Venera we cross the Valle della Vena and farther on the Valle delle Forche.

Mount Piedmonte Etneo (1140 ft.) Carriage from Taormina, is a small town situated on the old military road from Palermo to Messina, which the railway now follows, first towards the north west and then towards the west as far as Randazzo. Himilco followed this route in B.C. 396, Timoleon in B.C. 344, and Charles V. in 1534 A.D. To the left rises Mount Ætna, to the right the wooded slopes of Monte Calciniera (2650 ft.). The line crosses several torrents, which are generally dry in summer. Between (10½ miles) Terremorte and (12½ miles) Linguaglossa, the remains of the eruption of 1566 are traversed. Higher up the mountain is the Pineta di Linguaglossa, a large pine-grove.

Castiglione, 3½ miles to the south of the high-lying little town of Castiglione di Sicilia (2035 ft. 12,272 inhabitants to Francavilla), which yields the best Sicilian hazelnuts. Farther on, we obtain a view of the valley of the Alcantara, to the right, above which rises the chain of the lofty Nebrodi.

Mount Solicchiata – between Moio, with the northern-most crater of the Ætna district, and Calderara (già Merenda) we traverse part of the lava ejected by Mount Ætna in 1879 which may be conveniently visited from Randazzo. The lava advanced nearly as far as the Alcántara, and threatened to overwhelm the village of Moio, situated 3 miles to the north east of the station, the inhabitants of which sought to appease the wrath of nature by a religious procession bearing the statue of St. Anthony, their patron saint.

The section between Randazzo and Bronte is the finest part of the railway round Mount Ætna. The line still ascends, at first through a forest of oaks. The culture of the ground assumes quite a northern character. After traversing a bleak field of lava we reach the watershed between the Alcantara and Simeto (3810 ft.) a little short of Maletto, a small town with an old castle, on the slope of the conical hill of the same name. The torrents in spring form the small lake Gurrita to the right, the exhalations from which poison the atmosphere in summer.

(From *Italy, Part 3: Southern Italy and Sicily, with Excursions into the Liparia Islands, Malta, Sardinia, Tunis, and Corfu*; Karl Baedeker, 1903)

Railways in France, 1907

Karl Baedeker

Baedeker understood that some people – probably mainly men – wanted to know 'how it works'. It is also indicated by Baedeker that French railways were, in some form, nationalised as long ago as 1898 …

The network of railways with which France is now overspread consists of lines of an aggregate length of 20,300 miles, belonging to the Government, in six large companies, and in a larger number of smaller ones.

The fares per English mile are approximately: first class 18 centimes, second class 12 centimes, third class 8 centimes, to which a tax of ten per cent on each ticket costing more than 10 francs is added. The mail trains generally convey first class passengers only, and the express trains first class and second class passengers only.

The first class carriages are good, but the second class carriages are inferior to those in most other parts of Europe and the third class are not always furnished with cushioned seats. The trains are generally provided with smoking carriages, and in others smoking is allowed unless any one of the passengers objects. Ladies compartments are also provided.

The trains invariably pass each other on the left, so that the traveller can always tell which side of a station his train starts from. The speed of the express trains is about 35 to 45 miles per hour, but that of the ordinary trains is often very much less.

Travellers must purchase their tickets before entering the

waiting rooms, but, contrary to the custom in other parts of France, they are then permitted free access to the platform, and may choose their own seats in the train. Tickets for intermediate stations are usually collected at the '*sortie*'; those for termini, before the station is entered.

Travellers within France are allowed 30 kilograms (66 English pounds) of luggage free of charge; those who are bound for foreign countries are allowed 25 kilograms only (55 pounds). In all cases the heavier luggage must be booked, and a ticket procured for it; this being done the traveller need not enquire after his 'impediments' until he arrives and presents his ticket at his final destination. Where however a frontier has to be crossed, the traveller should see his luggage cleared at the customs house in person. At most of the railway stations there is a *consigne* – or left luggage office, where a charge of 10 centimes a day is made for one or two packages, and five centimes a day for each additional article.

Where there is no *consigne*, the employees will generally take care of luggage for a trifling fee.

The railway porters (*factuers*) are not entitled to remuneration, but it is usual to give a few sous for their services. Interpreters are found at most of the larger stations.

There are no refreshment rooms (*buffets*) except at the principal stations; and as the viands are generally indifferent, the charges high, and the stoppages brief, the traveller is advised to provide himself beforehand with the necessary sustenance and consume it at his leisure in the railway carriage.

Sleeping carriages (*wagons lits*) are provided on nearly all the lines of the great railway systems. Trains de luxe with dining room, sleeping and drawing room cars (*wagon restaurants*) run on certain days during the season – to Nice via Lyons and Marseilles and to Geneva (via Macon) . Pillows and rugs may be hired at the appropriate stations.

(From *Paris and environs, with routes from London to Paris*; Karl Baedeker, 1907)

Too often travel, instead of broadening the mind,

The Direct-Orient Express, 1975

Paul Theroux

The author spent four months travelling across Europe and Asia by train, taking the Direct-Orient Express from Paris to Istanbul. This was not the luxurious special train laid on for rich tourists but the through-carriages that get attached to other services across Europe.

Duffill had put on a pair of glasses, wire-framed and with enough Scotch tape on the lenses to prevent his seeing the Blue Mosque. He assembled his parcels and, grunting, produced a suitcase, bound with a selection of leather and canvas belts as an added guarantee against it bursting open. A few cars down we met again to read the sign on the side of the wagon-lit: DIRECT-ORIENT and its itinerary, PARIS – LAUSANNE – MILANO – TRIESTE – ZAGREB – BEOGRAD – SOFIYA – ISTANBUL. We stood there, staring at this sign; Duffill worked his glasses like binoculars. Finally he said, 'I took this train in nineteen twenty-nine.'

It seemed to call for a reply, but by the time a reply occurred to me ('Judging from its condition, it was probably this very train!') Duffill had gathered up his parcels and his strapped suit-case and moved down the platform. It was a great train in 1929, and it goes without saying that the Orient Express is the most famous train in the world.

☆ ☆ ☆

At 9.35 we stopped at the Italian station of Domodossola, where a man poured cups of coffee from a jug and sold food from a heavily laden pushcart. He had fruit, loaves of bread and rolls, various kinds of salami, and lunch bags that, he said, contained '*tante belle cose*'. He also had a stock of wine. Molesworth bought a Bardolino and ('just in case') three bottles of Chianti; I bought an Orvieto and a Chianti; and Duffill had his hand on a bottle of claret.

Molesworth said, 'I'll take these back to the compartment. 'Get me a lunch bag, will you?'

merely lengthens the conversation. Elizabeth Drew

I bought two lunch bags and some apples.

Duffill said, 'English money, I only have English money.' The Italian snatched a pound from the old man and gave him change in lire.

Molesworth came back and said, 'Those apples want washing. There's cholera here.' He looked again at the pushcart and said, 'I think *two* lunch bags, just to be safe.'

While Molesworth bought more food and another bottle of Bardolino, Duffill said, 'I took this train in nineteen twenty-nine'.

'It was worth taking then,' said Molesworth. 'Yes, she used to be quite a train'.

'How long are we staying here?' I asked.

No one knew. Molesworth called out to the train guard, 'I say, George, how long are we stopping for?'

The guard shrugged, and as he did so the train began to back up.

'Do you think we should board?' I asked.

'It's going backwards,' said Molesworth. 'I expect they're shunting.'

The train guard said, '*Andiamo*.'

'The Italians love wearing uniforms,' said Molesworth. 'Look at him, will you? And the uniforms are always so wretched. They really are like overgrown schoolboys. Are you talking to us, George?'

'I think he wants us to board,' I said. The train stopped going backwards. I hopped aboard and looked down. Molesworth and Duffill were at the bottom of the stairs.

'You've got parcels,' said Duffill. 'You go first.'

'I'm quite all right,' said Molesworth. 'Up you go.'

'But you've got parcels,' said Duffill. He produced a pipe from his coat and began sucking on the stem. 'Carry on.' He moved back and gave Molesworth room.

Molesworth said, 'Are you sure?'

Duffill said, 'I didn't go all the way, then, in nineteen twenty-nine. I didn't do that until after the second war'. He put his pipe in his mouth and smiled.

Molesworth stepped aboard and climbed up – slowly, because he was carrying a bottle of wine and his second lunch bag. Duffill grasped the rails beside the door and as he did so the train began to move and he let go. He dropped his arms. Two train guards rushed behind him and held his arms and hustled him along the platform to the moving stairs of Car 99. Duffill, feeling the Italians' hands, resisted the embrace, went feeble, and stepped back; he made a half-turn to smile wanly at the fugitive door. He looked a hundred years old. The train was moving swiftly past his face.

'George!' cried Molesworth. 'Stop the train!'

I was leaning out the door. I said, 'He's still on the platform.'

There were two Italians beside us, the conductor and a bed-maker. Their shoulders were poised, preparing to shrug.

'Pull the emergency cord !' said Molesworth.

'No, no, no, no,' said the conductor. 'If I pull that I must pay five thousand lire. Don't touch!'

'Is there another train?' I asked.

'*Si,*' said the bed-maker in a tone of irritation. 'He can catch us in Milano.'

'What time does the next train get to Milano?' I asked.

'Two o'clock.'

'When do we get to Milano?'

'One o'clock,' said the conductor. 'We leave at two.'

'Well, how the hell –'

'The old man can take a car,' explained the bed-maker. 'Don't worry. He hires a taxi at Domodossola; the taxi goes *varooom*! He's in Milano before us!'

Molesworth said, 'These chaps could use a few lessons in how to run a railroad.'

it's not a freight train! MARIAH CAREY

The meal that followed the abandoning of Duffill only made that point plainer. It was a picnic in Molesworth's compartment; we were joined by the Belgian girl, Monique, who brought her own cheese. She asked for mineral water and got Molesworth's reprimand: 'Sorry, I keep that for my teeth.' We sat shoulder to shoulder on Molesworth's bed, gloomily picking through our lunch bags.

'I wasn't quite prepared for this,' said Molesworth. 'I think each country should have its own dining car. Shunt it on at the frontier and serve slap-up meals.' He nibbled a hard-boiled egg and said, 'Perhaps we should get together and write a letter to Cook's.'

The Orient Express, once unique for its service, is now unique among trains for its lack of it.

(From *The Great Railway Bazaar*; Penguin, 1977, © Paul Theroux)

The train is a small world moving through a larger world.
ELISHA COOPER

ASIA

3

The Post Train, 1900

ANNETTE MEAKIN

On a visit to Russia in 1896 Annette Meakin became 'seized with a desire not merely to make the journey on the Trans-Siberian Railway, but to be the first Englishwoman to travel by that route to Japan'. She set off on 18th March 1900 taking with her a valise and hold-all, a tea-basket and her elderly mother ...

We had not been long in Siberia before we knew from experience that the only way to enjoy life was to give ourselves over entirely to a state of blissful uncertainty about everything in the future. If people told us when a train would arrive or when a steamer would start, they invariably told us wrong. Any information gleaned in one town about another to which we were going was sure to be flatly contradicted on our arrival. Of course this could be partly accounted for by the great distances. When a town is separated from its nearest neighbour by a railway journey, say, of two nights and three days, it certainly has some excuse on its side. Still, after having made your home for several days in a comfortable railway carriage, or yet more comfortable house boat, it is somewhat trying to arrive without warning at your destination several hours before you expected to get there, or to have to unpack and spend another night in a carriage you had expected to leave at midday.

We left Omsk by the post train which ought to have started at 9.30 p.m., according to the time table. It was only four hours late, a mere nothing in Siberia, where time is not money. As we sat waiting at the station the good news was brought us that Mafeking had been relieved. The bearer of these tidings was the Finnish Pastor, who had only an hour before received word by telegram from Finland. The Finns have all along shown great sympathy with the English with regard to the Transvaal war. Pastor Erikson met us with a hearty handshake and a beaming face. A burst of military music close at hand seemed very opportune to our English ears. We looked out and saw a pretty sight. Under the bright electric light on the platform from which we were to start gleamed the white hats and jackets of some thirty bandsmen. Their music was in honour of the colonel of their regiment, who, after a period of twenty-four years' service at Omsk, was leaving with his family for a better appointment at Irkutsk.

The train seemed to carry music with it as it glided into the station, and the crowded platform was a whirl of gaiety and excitement. All this in the middle of the night! We found our *coupé* on the post train not less comfortable than the one we had occupied on the express. The cushions were all covered with neat washing covers, and looked tolerably clean. Under the window was a little folding table which was most useful for reading and writing. I speak of *the* window because there was only a window at one end of the carriage. Like the express, the post is also a corridor train. The door opening into the corridor had a mirror in place of a window; it opened outwards and could be fastened back against the outer wall when we wished to travel with it open. The mirror was useless when the door was shut, as one stood in one's own light when looking into it. We occasionally went out into the corridor to complete our toilette when a glass was indispensable. This however was not so bad as in Canada, where I have seen a gentleman shaving in the public 'sleeper.' The corridor was so wide that the stoutest traveller could promenade in it with ease. On wet days we could get a walk here of about twenty-five paces; seats could be opened out from the walls between the windows as in the express, and passengers used to congregate here in the evenings when it was too dark to read.

The post train has no dining car, and we were obliged to keep a sharp look out for stations where there was something to eat. The first day after leaving Omsk we passed a buffet station about 11 a.m., but being asleep, did not take advantage of it.

One's destination is never a place, but

'You must be hungry,' said a fellow passenger pityingly about seven in the evening; 'but we shall reach Kainsk in about an hour, and there is a good buffet there.' Just then the train began to pull up. It soon came to a dead stop. There was no human habitation in sight.

'The engine has smashed up,' said a jolly Russian sailor in broken English, (he was bound for Port Arthur). 'She is sixty years old,' he continued. 'She was made in Glasgow. She is no use any more.'

The conductor had got out. He came along the line and confirmed what the sailor had said. The other passengers did not seem to mind; they were soon exploring the neighbourhood. The children from the fourth class began to paddle barefoot in a muddy stream not far from the line. The poor old engine was now towed to her last berth.' I had whipped out my 'Kodak' and taken her photograph thinking of Turner's 'Fighting Temeraire.'

After a delay of two hours a fresh engine arrived from Kainsk and we reached the buffet at last. Never again, we vowed, would we be subject to such pangs of hunger as we suffered that day; in future we took care to have some food always with us, if it was only a loaf of bread. The serving man was willing for a few kopeks to fetch us hot water at the stations, so that with the help of bread and tea there was no need to starve.

(From *A Ribbon of Iron*; Constable, 1901)

Trans-Siberian Tales, 1922

LESLEY BLANCH

Lesley Blanch's 'Journey into the Mind's Eye' is one of the first books that came into my hands before I set off on the journey myself and I, as have many others, found it inspirational. Her obsession for the journey began at a very young age, fuelled by the tales of a family friend, to whom she refers as the 'Traveller'.

The Traveller had come to rest in the rocking-chair. The clumsy folds of his great fur-lined overcoat stood round him like a box, while a number of scarves tangled under his chin. His tight skinned Chinese-yellow face seemed to glow, incandescent, in the light of the nursery fire where we made beef-dripping toast together. Even this warming occupation could not persuade him to remove his overcoat.

'You'll catch your death of cold when you go out,' my nurse would always say. 'Not after Siberia,' the Traveller would always reply. It was a ritual.

Of all the lands he had known, his own, Russia, seemed to me the most fabulous. He was from Moscow, 'a Muscovite', he said, but later I was to learn he was of Tartar blood; and unmistakably, the Ta-tze or Mongol hordes had stamped their imprint on his strange countenance. The dark slit eyes, the pointed ears, the bald, Chinese-bald skull, the slight, yet cruel smile which sometimes passed across his usually impassive face – all these spoke of Asia, of the Golden Horde, and the limitless horizons of Central Asia, where he roamed, in spirit, and in fact.

Whenever he came to Europe, he would visit us, and then, reaching my nursery, sit beside the fire, his huge shadow spread-eagled – a double-headed Russian eagle to me – across the rosy wall-paper. Shrugging and gesticulating with odd, unexpected movements, his long, bent-back fingers cracking, the nail of one little finger sprouted to astonishing length, he would spin a marvellous web of countries, cities, people and things, conjuring for me a world of shimmering images.

☆ ☆ ☆

Sometimes he told me fairy stories – Russian legends, Uya Mourametz the heroic, or Konyiok Gorbunok, the little hump-backed horse who brought his master such good fortune; or the magical cat, chained to a tree, who sang verses when he circled to the right, and told fairy tales when he went to the left ... Best of all, he would tell of the great train that ran half across the world – the most luxurious and splendid train that ever was – the Trans-Siberian.

He held me enthralled then, and today, a life-time later, the spell still holds. He told me the train's history, its beginnings (first mooted, it seemed, by an Englishman, a Mr. Dull by name); how

There's something about the sound of a train that's

a Tzar had said, 'Let the Railway be built!' And it was. He told me of its mileage, five thousand (to the Canadian-Pacific's three thousand); of its splendours: brass bedsteads instead of bunks; libraries, hot baths, and grand pianos to while away the hours. (From Moscow to Irkutsk, barely a half way point to Vladivostok, was nearly a week's travelling.) Of its miseries; of prison wagons, iron barred trucks hitched on at some wayside halt where the shackled lines of wretched creatures could be heard clanking their chains, often five pounds of wooden logs added to the heavy irons – and singing their traditional exiles' begging song, the Miloserdnaya, a sort of funeral chant of doom and despair.

'How did they learn it?' I asked. His face changed terribly. Another mask, of pure hatred, suddenly succeeded the habitual one of Asiatic impassivity.

'Those who went on foot sometimes took over a year to reach Tiumen – not even half-way,' he said, 'two miles an hour – twenty miles a day was good going in chains ... They had plenty of time to learn the begging song. And to learn how to suffer, and die,' he added. He shrugged. 'Life teaches.' It was one of his favourite dictums. Then, wrenching himself from Siberia to London, he became suddenly autocratic. 'More tea!' he demanded, and I hurried to the tea-pot.

He always insisted on having his tea, Russian-style, in a glass. He liked a spoonful of cherry jam in the saucer, beside it. Sometimes he showed me how the peasants held a lump of sugar in their teeth, and sucked the tea through it, noisily, for sugar was a great luxury among them, and not to be dissolved prematurely. The Traveller always drank his own tea in a strange fashion. He never held the glass in his hand, but would leave it on the table, then bend his head down to it, rather like a camel drinking. And all the while his wicked-glinting little eyes would range round the room. If anything so narrow could be said to roll – they rolled ecstatically. He particularly savoured the China tea my mother obtained, and he strongly approved of her allowing it in the nursery. Even more, he admired her for giving me a beautiful old Worcester tea-cup for my own use.

'When I was your age, I drank from Tamerlaine's jade drinking cup,' he said, and I believed him.

How I loved him! How I loved his Traveller's tales and the way he brought the Trans-Siberian railway thundering through the house. There was a chapel on the train, he said; a candle-lit ikon-filled chapel where the long-haired, long-bearded Orthodox priests ('*Popes* we call them') gathered the pious together before a gilded iconotas, praying and swaying as the great engine snaked across the steppes. Piety ran the length of the train. Piety and patriotism: love of a country. As the train rattled across the bridge over the Volga, every man stood up and doffed his cap to Mother Volga.

I knew it all by heart. Every Wednesday and Saturday, the Trans-Siberian train pulled out of Moscow and for seven days ate up the eastward miles to Irkutsk, and farther, into the heart of Siberia, through the Trans-Baikal provinces, edging the Mongol steppes and the yellow dust-clouds of the Gobi desert. There was a branch line to Outer Mongolia – another, along the Amur, to bandit-infested Manchuria, and at last, ten days later – Vladivostok, Russian outlet of life and death on the Sea of Japan. One extension of the line led to the Forbidden City.

'The gates were scarlet lacquer, a hundred and fifty feet high and stuck with the heads of malefactors,' said the Traveller, spreading beef-dripping with a lavish hand.

☆ ☆ ☆

For me, nothing was ever the same again. I had fallen in love with the Traveller's travels. Gradually, I became possessed by love of a horizon and a train which would take me there; of a fabled engine and an imagined landscape, seen through a pair of narrowed eyes set slant-wise in a yellow Mongol face. These Asiatic wastes were to become, for me, the landscape of my heart, that secret landscape of longing which glides before our eyes between sleeping and waking; a region I could not fathom, but into which I was drawn, ever deeper, more voluptuously, till it became both a challenge and a retreat. It was another dimension where I could refuge from the rooms and streets about which I moved, docile but apart. From the first, the Traveller had understood my infatuation for Asia, and every time he came to see me, he brought some object which told of those horizons. A chunk of malachite, or a Kazakh fox-skin cap (which smelt rather rank) and once, a *bunchuk*, or standard, decorated with the dangling horse-tails of a Mongol chieftain. I was enraptured.

'Nasty dangerous thing,' said Nanny, holding it at arm's length and depositing it in the umbrella-stand. 'Why can't he bring you dolls, dressed up in national costumes? You could have quite a collection by now.'

But the Traveller knew better.

☆ ☆ ☆

Gradually, the Trans-Siberian journey became an obsession. But how to make it? At that time, my journeys were circumscribed: family holidays to Sussex downs or Cornish beaches (ginger-bread biscuits after an icy dip, sand-shoes drying on the window-sill, along with strips of sea-weed). But there were travel-books to comfort me, and whole worlds to be explored by turning the pages. The top shelf of my toy-cupboard turned bookcase now assumed a most business-like air, and was labelled SIBERIA, while I waited for donations. I had learned to read very young, so that by seven I was experimenting with any book I could lay hands on. When my father, who believed in children reading anything, at any age, cynically produced Dostoievsky's *House of the Dead* my mother suggested Jules Verne's *Michel Strogoff* would have been more suitable, to which my father replied that he had no doubt wading through Dostoievsky's miseries would finish my Siberian craze for good. My mother contributed Xavier de Maistre's *La Jeune Sibérienne*, in the hope it would improve my French, while Aunt Ethel produced Harry de Windt's fearful accounts of a journey across Arctic Siberia, among the convict settlements and political prisoners. But still my enthusiasm grew.

☆ ☆ ☆

'Siberia! I'll give you Siberia – you with your chilblains,' said my nurse, when I whined to go out in the brown-edged, slushy London snow. I was hardening myself: in preparation for journeys to Omsk and Tomsk (later I named two kittens after these

so fast that people can't get on board. HV MORTON

towns) and the mysterious, icy-sounding places along the Trans-Siberian's way. Verkhne-Udinsk, Chita and Chailor Gol were names round which the tempests of Asia howled. Nevertheless Nanny, who had now left us, showed an understanding of my peculiar passion, and next Christmas sent me a purple-bound volume (a come-by chance, off a barrow in the Portobello Road) entitled *On Sledge and Horse-back to the Outcast Siberian Lepers* by Kate Marsden – New York 1892.

'Must have been off her rocker,' said cook, when I read her the more dramatic passages. Moreover she was adamant in her refusal to make *pelmeni*, pieces of stuffed pasta, a celebrated Tartar dish, of which the Traveller had given me the recipe.

'Staple Siberian diet,' he said. 'Filthy, but filling.' He also added it was very hard to make.

'Which is as maybe,' said cook darkly, basting the roast in a crimson glow of professional complacency.

Nor was she any more co-operative when I dwelled on the habits of Jenghis Khan's troops who were required to carry a sheep's stomach full of desiccated dried meat, and another of powdered milk flour under their saddles, thus being ever at the ready to gallop off on some foray.

'But it would only be like getting a haggis,' I pleaded, when she refused to supply a sheep's stomach. I had planned to attach it to my tricycle, and thus provided, pedal furiously off down the path to Asia.

(From *Journey into the Mind's Eye*; Century, 1987, © Lesley Blanch)

Life aboard the Trans-Siberian, 1933

PETER FLEMING

As a correspondent for 'The Times', Peter Fleming (brother of Ian Fleming) travelled widely and wrote several books of his journeys. In One's Company he describes his rail trip from London to Moscow and then on to China aboard the Trans-Siberian.

Everyone is a romantic, though in some the romanticism is of a perverted and paradoxical kind. And for a romantic it is, after all,

The world's longest train journey without requiring a change

something to stand in the sunlight beside the Trans-Siberian Express with the casually proprietorial air of the passenger, and to reflect that that long raking chain of steel and wood and glass is to go swinging and clattering out of the West into the East, carrying you with it. The metals curve glinting into the distance, a slender bridge between two different worlds. In eight days you will be in Manchuria. Eight days of solid travel: none of those spectacular but unrevealing leaps and bounds which the aeroplane, that agent of superficiality to-day, makes possible. The arrogance of the hardbitten descends on you. You recall your friends in England, whom only the prospect of shooting grouse can reconcile to eight hours in the train without complaint. Eight *hours* indeed... you smile contemptuously.

Besides, the dignity, or at least the glamour of trains has lately been enhanced. *Shanghai Express, Rome Express, Stamboul Train* – these and others have successfully exploited its potentialities as a setting for adventure and romance. In fiction, drama, and the films there has been a firmer tone in Wagons Lits than ever since the early days of Oppenheim. Complacently you weigh your chances of a foreign countess, the secret emissary of a Certain Power, her corsage stuffed with documents of the first political importance. Will anyone mistake you for No. 37, whose real name no one knows, and who is practically always in a train, being 'whirled' somewhere? You have an intoxicating vision of drugged liqueurs, rifled dispatch-cases, lights suddenly extinguished, and door-handles turning slowly under the bright eye of an automatic... .

You have this vision, at least, if you have not been that way before. I had. For me there were no thrills of discovery and anticipation. One hears of time standing still; in my case it took two paces smartly to the rear. As I settled down in my compartment, and the train pulled out through shoddy suburbs into a country clothed in birch and fir, the unreal rhythm of train-life was resumed as though it had never been broken. The nondescript smell of the upholstery, the unrelenting rattle of our progress, the tall glass of weak tea in its metal holder, the unshaven jowls and fatuous but friendly smile of the little attendant who brought it –

is the twice monthly through-coach Moscow to Pyongyang (10,175 km) which takes 210 hours 20 minutes.

all these unmemorable components of a former routine, suddenly resurrected, blotted out the interim between this journey and the last. The inconsequent comedy of two years, with the drab or coloured places, the cities and the forests, where it had been played, became for a moment as though it had never been. This small, timeless, moving cell I recognized as my home and my doom. I felt as if I had always been on the Trans-Siberian Express.

The dining-car was certainly unchanged. On each table there still ceremoniously stood two opulent black bottles of some unthinkable wine, false pledges of conviviality. They were never opened, and rarely dusted. They may contain ink, they may contain the elixir of life. I do not know. I doubt if anyone does.

Lavish but faded paper frills still clustered coyly round the pots of paper flowers, from whose sad petals the dust of two continents perpetually threatened the specific gravity of the soup. The lengthy and trilingual menu had not been revised; 75 per cent of the dishes were still apocryphal, all the prices were exorbitant. The cruet, as before, was of interest rather to the geologist than to the gourmet. Coal dust from the Donetz Basin, tiny flakes of granite from the Urals, sand whipped by the wind all the way from the Gobi Desert – what a fascinating story that salt-cellar could have told under the microscope. Nor was there anything different about the attendants. They still sat in huddled cabal at the far end of the car, conversing in low and disillusioned tones, while the *chef du train*, a potent gnome-like man, played on his abacus a slow significant tattoo. Their surliness went no deeper than the grime upon their faces; they were always ready to be amused by one's struggles with the language or the cooking. Sign-language they interpreted with more eagerness than apprehension: as when my desire for a hard-boiled egg – no easy request, when you come to think of it, to make in pantomime – was fulfilled, three-quarters of an hour after it had been expressed, by the appearance of a whole roast fowl.

The only change of which I was aware was in my stable-companion. Two years ago it had been a young Australian, a man much preoccupied with the remoter contingencies of travel. 'Supposing', he would muse, 'the train breaks down, will there

To many people holidays are not voyages of discovery,

be danger of attack by wolves?' When he undressed he panted fiercely, as though wrestling with the invisible Fiend; he had a plaintive voice, and on his lips the words 'nasal douche'(the mere sound of Siberia had given him a cold) had the saddest cadence you can imagine. This time it was a young Russian, about whom I remember nothing at all. Nor is this surprising, for I never found out anything about him. He spoke no English, and I spoke hardly any Russian. A phrase-book bought in Moscow failed to bridge the gap between us. An admirable compilation in many ways, it did not, I discovered, equip one for casual conversation with a stranger. There was a certain petulance, a touch of the imperious and exorbitant, about such observations as: 'Show me the manager, the assistant manager, the water closet, Lenin's Tomb', and 'Please to bring me tea, coffee, beer, vodka, cognac, Caucasian red wine, Caucasian white wine'. Besides, a lot of the questions, like 'Can you direct me to the Palace of the Soviets?' and 'Why must I work for a World Revolution?' were not the sort of things I wanted to ask him; and most of the plain statements of fact – such as 'I am an American engineer who loves Russia' and 'I wish to study Architecture, Medicine, Banking under the best teachers, please' – would have been misleading. I did not want to mislead him.

So for two days we grinned and nodded and got out of each other's way and watched each other incuriously, in silence. On the second day he left the train, and after that I had the compartment to myself.

There is a great deal to be said against trains, but it will not be said by me. I like the Trans-Siberian Railway. It is a confession of weakness, I know; but it is sincere.

You wake up in the morning. Your watch says its eight o'clock; but you are travelling east, and you know that it is really nine, though you might be hard put to it to explain why this is so. Your berth is comfortable. There is no need to get up, and no incentive either. You have nothing to look forward to, nothing to avoid. No assets, no liabilities. Most men, though not the best men, are happiest when the question 'What shall I do?' is supererogatory. (Hence the common and usually just contention that 'My schooldays were the happiest days of my life'.) That is

but a ritual of reassurance. PHILIP ANDREW ADAMS

why I like the Trans-Siberian Railway. You lie in your berth, justifiably inert. Past the window plains crawl and forests flicker. The sun shines weakly on an empty land. The piles of birch logs by the permanent way – silver on the outside, black where the damp butts show – give the anomalous illusion that there has been a frost. There is always a magpie in sight.

You have nothing to look at, but no reason to stop looking. You are living in a vacuum, and at last you have to invent some absurdly artificial necessity for getting up: 'fifteen magpies from now', or 'next time the engine whistles'. For you are inwardly afraid that without some self-discipline to give it a pattern this long period of suspended animation will permanently affect your character for the worse.

So in the end you get up, washing perfunctorily in the little dark confessional which you share with the next compartment, and in the basin for which the experienced traveller brings his own plug, because the Russians, for some reason connected – strangely enough – with religion, omit to furnish these indispensable adjuncts to a careful toilet.

Then, grasping your private pot of marmalade, you lurch along to the dining-car. It is now eleven o'clock, and the dining-car is empty.

You order tea and bread, and make without appetite a breakfast which is more than sufficient for your needs. The dining-car is almost certainly stuffier, but you have ceased to notice this. The windows are always shut, either because the weather is cold, or because it is warm and dry and therefore dusty. (Not, of course, that the shutting of them excludes the dust. Far from it. But it is at least a gesture; it is the best that can be done.)

After that you wander back to your compartment. The provodnik has transformed your bed into a seat, and perhaps you hold with him some foolish conversation, in which the rudiments of three languages are prostituted in an endeavor to compliment each other on their simultaneous mastery. Then you sit down and read. You read and read and read. There are no distractions, no interruptions, no temptations to get up and do something else; there is nothing else to do. You read as you have never read before.

If you reject the food, ignore the customs, fear the religion

And so the day passes. If you are wise you shun the regulation meal at three o'clock, which consists of five courses not easily to be identified, and during which the car is crowded and the windows blurred with steam. I had brought with me from London biscuits and potted meat and cheese; and he is a fool who does not take at least some victuals of his own. But as a matter of fact, what with the airless atmosphere and the lack of exercise, you don't feel hungry on the Trans-Siberian Railway. A pleasant lassitude, a sense almost of disembodiment, descends on you, and the food in the dining-car which, though seldom really bad, is never appetizing and sometimes scarce, hardly attracts that vigorous criticism which it would on a shorter journey.

At the more westerly stations – there are perhaps three stops of twenty minutes every day – you pace the platforms vigorously, in a conscientious British way. But gradually this practice is abandoned. As you are drawn further into Asia, old fetishes lose their power. It becomes harder and harder to persuade yourself that you feel a craving for exercise, and indeed you almost forget that you ought to feel this craving. At first you are alarmed, for this is the East, the notorious East, where white men go to pieces; you fear that you are losing your grip, that you are going native. But you do nothing about it, and soon your conscience ceases to prick and it seems quite natural to stand limply in the sunlight, owlish, frowsty, and immobile, like everybody else.

At last evening comes. The sun is setting somewhere far back along the road that you have travelled. A slanting light always lends intimacy to a landscape, and this Siberia, flecked darkly by the tapering shadows of trees, seems a place at once more friendly and more mysterious than the naked non-committal flats of noon. Your eyes are tired, and you put down your book. Against the grey and creeping distances outside memory and imagination stage in their turn the struggles of the past and of the future. For the first time loneliness descends, and you sit examining its implications until you find Siberia vanished and the grimy window offering nothing save your own face, foolish, indistinct, and as likely as not unshaved. You adjourn to the dining-car, for eggs.

(From *One's Company*; Cape, 1936, © Peter Fleming)

and avoid the people, you might better stay home.
JAMES MICHENER

The Big Red Train Ride, 1977

ERIC NEWBY

In 1977 Eric Newby and his wife Wanda travelled across the USSR on the Trans-Siberian Railway from Moscow to the Pacific with an official guide and a photographer. Through his resulting book, 'The Big Red Train Ride', he has provided a splendidly entertaining description of travel as a tourist in a communist country.

Now the *Rossiya* was running off the bridge, which was guarded, as are all the bigger bridges and all the tunnels on the Railway – this one by a very small sentry in a very large greatcoat, who looked as if he could do with a spring clean, and who was giving himself an airing outside his sentry box, a sight that would have cheered the Pentagon. From here I could look down the embankment on to the low-lying Meadow Bank of the river, on to orchards, fields of what looked like heavy brown clay which was sown with something, probably potatoes or flax, and on to the rooftops of wooden houses which were painted in shades of ochre, ginger and the same dark brown as the earth: a scene that a few moments ago would have been gloomy in the extreme, now transformed by the brilliant early afternoon sun. Could it be that spring had really come at last?

Chekhov too took a less jaundiced view of Russia as soon as the weather took a turn for the better. In April 1890 when he was travelling, there was no through road to the Urals and work on the Trans-Siberian had not yet begun. Instead, after he had reached Yaroslavl, he boarded a steamer to go to Kazan, where he boarded yet another steamer which took him to Perm.

On waking I saw the sun (Chekhov wrote to his sister). The Volga is not bad: water meadows, sun-drenched monasteries, white churches, an amazing expanse; wherever you look it's cosy, inviting you to sit down and cast a line . . . now and then a shepherd's horn is heard. White seagulls hover over the Volga....

'What I want to know,' I said to Mischa (never one to let sleeping dogs lie), 'is why your government gets so steamed up about bridges. This book I've got describes every bridge on the

I wanted to invent an engine that could run for ever. I could
It would have looked like the

Trans-Siberian Railway in detail, and there are photographs of all the really big ones. I know we're not in Siberia yet; but I bet there's another book with pictures of all the bridges on the way to the Urals. Anyway, what difference does it make? They all get photographed from satellites.' .

'I have never seen such a book,' he said.

'Well, would you like to look at it? Here!'

'I do not want to look at it.'

'Well, just listen to this then: 'At the 1328 verst* the line crosses the river.'

'Which river?'

'The Ob. Would you mind if I get on with it, as it's rather long?'

'The line crosses the river by a bridge 372.50 sahzens* long having seven spans. The I and VI openings are 46.325 sahzens, the II, IV, 53.65 sahzens, and III and V, 53.15 sahzens. The upper girders of the bridge are on the Herber's system.'

I'm going to cut it short. 'The stone abutments of the bridge are laid on granite rocks, the right pier, No. 1, near the bank is not supported on a caisson, the other piers, Nos. 2, 3, 4, 5 and 6 are laid on caissons sunk to a depth of 1.81 to 3.40 sahzens below the lowest water level. The minimum elevation of the trusses above the low water mark is 8.23 sahzens and 4.42 above its highest level ...

'Look, there's an awful lot more: you don't want me to go on do you? It's terribly boring.'

'You should not be in possession of such a book,' said Mischa, severely. 'Such a book is a confidential publication.'

'But this is the official Russian guide to the Trans-Siberian Railway, published in English in 1900. And it's a reprint. I bought it in Britain a couple of weeks ago. Look, it's even got a picture of the Boss.' And I tried to show him the frontispiece, a photograph of that supreme twit His Majesty Nicholas Alexandrovich, Autocrat of All the Russias, Most August President of the Committee of the Siberian Railway, without whose untiring efforts to bring about the Revolution I would probably not have been sitting here on the Rossiya arguing with Mischa.

'You should not have brought this book into the country. You

have developed a new train, had I stayed in the railway. AK-47 though. MIKHAIL KALASHNIKOV

should have declared it to the Customs authorities.'

(A facsimile of the *Guide to the Great Siberian Railway*, first published in St Petersburg in 1900, has been published by David and Charles of Newton Abbot, Devon, which is how I came to acquire it, it being otherwise a rare work.)

'No one asked us to declare anything. We've got *Vogue, Harper's and Queen*, the *Observer, Sunday Times, Sunday Telegraph, The Times, Guardian, Time Magazine, Italian Panorama* and *Country Life*. We thought you'd be interested. Anyway, it was you who took us through Customs.'

'You shouldn't have all those either.'

'That's a fine thing to say when I've already given you my *Observer*.'

* 1 verst = 0.663 mile; 3500 feet; 1 sahzen = 7 feet

(From *The Big Red Train Ride*; Penguin, 1980, © Eric Newby)

Military Secrets, 1977

ERIC NEWBY

The car opposite our own on the other train was occupied by soldiers, and from our compartment we had an unprecedented view of its lavatory accommodation through its window which, unlike the lavatory windows on any other Russian train I had ever seen, or on any other train anywhere else in the world I had ever seen, was made of clear glass.

Both trains left a little late and in the course of the next few minutes we were treated to the extraordinary spectacle of a succession of Russian soliders each one of whom, on entering the lavatory, stood astride the pan and, as if he was performing a drill movement, lowered his trousers, in doing so revealing one of the most closely guarded military secrets of the Soviet Union – that its soldiers, like those of the kilted, Highland regiments in the British Army, are not issued with underpants. If this is a calumny and they are issued with underpants, then they had forgotten to put them on.

(From *The Big Red Train Ride*; Penguin, 1980, © Eric Newby)

I have found out that there ain't no surer way to find out

On the Siberian Railway, 1999

COLIN THUBRON

Colin Thubron did not always enjoy his journey. A great part of one's feelings about a journey as long as this depends upon one's companions en route. I had a good friend and some entertaining other travellers when I made this journey across the Soviet Union; Thubron did not …

Over the Urals the train wheels putter pathetically, like old men running out of breath. The mountains look too shallow to form a frontier, let alone the divide between Europe and Asia: only a faint upheaval of pine-darkened slopes.

Beyond my window the palisades of conifer and birch part to disclose sleepy villages and little towns by weed-smeared pools. The summer railway banks are glazed with flowers. Beyond them the clearings shut on and off like lantern slides: wooden cottages and vegetable patches boxed in picket fences, and cattle asleep in the grass.

Dusk suddenly, as if this were the frontier also between light and darkness. Siberia is only a few miles away. It sets up a tingle of alarm. I am sliding out of European Russia into somewhere that seems less a country than a region in people's minds, and even at this last moment, everything ahead – the violences of geography and time – feels a little thinned, too cold or vast to be precisely real. It impends through the darkness as the ultimate, unearthly Abroad. The place from which you will not return.

I chose it against my will. I was subverted by the sudden falling open of a vast area of the forbidden world. The immensity of Siberia that shadowed all my Asian journeys. So the casual beginnings – the furtive glances in an atlas – began to nag and deepen, until the wilderness seemed less to be empty than overlooked, or scrawled with invisible ink. Insidiously, it began to infect me.

The Azeri merchant who shares my carriage never looks out of the window. Siberia is dull, he says, and poor. He trades clothes between Moscow and Omsk, and taps continually on a

whether you like people or hate them than to travel with them.
MARK TWAIN

pocket calculator. 'I wouldn't stay long out there,' he says. 'Everything's falling to bits. I'd try China if I were you. China's the coming place.'

☆ ☆ ☆

Suddenly, in our window, there springs up the ghostly obelisk raised by Czar Alexander nearly two centuries ago. It stands on a low bank, whitened by the glimmer of our train. Here, geographically, Siberia begins. On its near side the plinth proclaims 'Europe', on its far side 'Asia'.

So I wait for the change I know will not happen. In the dark the railway cuttings seem to plunge deeper, and the trees to rush up more vertiginously above them. A few suffocated stars appear. Occasionally the land breaks into valleys slung with faint lights and, once, from the restaurant car, I see a horizon blanched with the refracted glow of an invisible city.

I don't sleep. The Azeri's snores thunder a yard from my head …

☆ ☆ ☆

My compartment was monopolised by a Ukrainian porter who sprawled out opposite his wife and sometimes stretched out a tattooed arm to pinch her cheek. Around us the bunks were occupied by sleeping Buryat girls, stacked up like dolls, who seemed more delicately in transit than the Russians. I felt I had grown invisible to them all: a down-at-heel Estonian. My boots now squealed as if they enclosed mice, but my snow-proof trousers and quilted jacket, I imagined, edged me into anonymity.

I knew these trains by heart now: their bossy attendant *provodnitsi*, their clamped windows, their stench of urine, raw fish, sweat. I too now softened dry noodles with scalding water from the carriage boiler, brewed up cheap coffee and picked at salted omul as the train and the hours crawled on. At dusk I lay curled up on an upper bunk reading a biography of Kolchak. A foot above my head a thin, unsteady graffito confided, 'Alya and Alyosha equals love.' Then the dark came down.

I think that travel comes from some deep
brings up a worm in an Irish bog to see

I tried to sleep. Somewhere beyond Chita the Trans-Manchurian Railway diverged south east through China. An imperial venture forced on the Chinese in 1896 – war-torn and bandit-ridden – it has completed the Trans-Siberian's link to the Pacific. It was this line, and the track where we travelled, that the White warlord, Grigory Semyenov, terrorised with gangs of Cossacks, Chinese brigands and Japanese mercenaries, riding the rails in armoured trains named 'The Destroyer' and 'The Terrible'.

Long after midnight we stopped at Nerchinsk, in whose silver mines Decembrists and Polish patriots had died, and in the darkness I missed the mouth of the Onon valley, birthplace of Genghis Khan. In its upper reaches, after a ravaged childhood, the conqueror gathered beneath him a fateful union of tribes, and in times of crisis would return to pray to the Sky God on the mountain at the river's source. But I looked out on blackness ...

☆ ☆ ☆

I got off the train at midnight into piercing cold. In the near empty station somebody said there was a hotel on the far side of the tracks, and I crossed a crumbling iron bridge and dropped into darkness .... .

(From *In Siberia;* Penguin, 2000, © Colin Thubron)

Calcutta to Darjeeling, 1896

MARK TWAIN

By February 1896, on his lecture tour of the British Empire, Mark Twain had reached India and took a rail trip to visit the fashionable Himalayan hill station, Darjeeling. He found his unorthodox form of rail transport most pleasurable.

Some time during the forenoon, approaching the mountains, we changed from the regular train to one composed of little canvas-sheltered cars that skimmed along within a foot of the ground and seemed to be going fifty miles an hour when they were really making about twenty. Each car had seating capacity for half-a-dozen persons; and when the curtains were up one was substantially out of doors, and could see everywhere, and get all the breeze, and be luxuriously comfortable. It was not a pleasure excursion in name only, but in fact.

After a while we stopped at a little wooden coop of a station just within the curtain of the sombre jungle, a place with a deep and dense forest of great trees and scrub and vines all about it. The royal Bengal tiger is in great force there, and is very bold and unconventional. From this lonely little station a message once went to the railway manager in Calcutta: 'Tiger eating stationmaster on front porch; telegraph instructions.'

It was there that I had my first tiger hunt. I killed thirteen. We were presently away again, and the train began to climb the mountains. In one place seven wild elephants crossed the track, but two of them got away before I could overtake them. The railway journey up the mountain is forty miles, and it takes eight hours to make it. It is so wild and interesting and exciting and enchanting that it ought to take a week. As for the vegetation, it is a museum. The jungle seemed to contain samples of every rare and curious tree and bush that we had ever seen or heard of. It is from that museum, I think, that the globe must have been supplied with the trees and vines and shrubs that it holds precious.

The road is infinitely and charmingly crooked. It goes winding in and out under lofty cliffs that are smothered in vines and foliage, and around the edges of bottomless chasms; and all the way one glides by files of picturesque natives, some carrying burdens up, others going down from their work in the tea-gardens; and once there was a gaudy wedding procession, all bright tinsel and color, and a bride, comely and girlish, who peeped out from the curtains of her palanquin, exposing her face with that pure delight which the young and happy take in sin for sin's own sake.

By and by we were well up in the region of the clouds, and from that breezy height we looked down and afar over a wonderful picture – the Plains of India, stretching to the horizon, soft and fair, level as a floor, shimmering with heat, mottled with cloud-shadows, and cloven with shining rivers. Immediately below us, and receding down, down, down, toward the valley,

Rail travel for me is the most relaxing, most scenic

was a shaven confusion of hilltops, with ribbony roads and paths squirming and snaking cream-yellow all over them and about them, every curve and twist sharply distinct.

At an elevation of 6,000 feet we entered a thick cloud, and it shut out the world and kept it shut out. We climbed 1,000 feet higher, then began to descend, and presently got down to Darjeeling, which is 6,000 feet above the level of the Plains.

☆ ☆ ☆

After lecturing I went to the Club that night, and that was a comfortable place. It is loftily situated, and looks out over a vast spread of scenery; from it you can see where the boundaries of three countries come together, some thirty miles away; Thibet is one of them, Nepaul another, and I think Herzegovina was the other. Apparently, in every town and city in India the gentlemen of the British civil and military service have a club; sometimes it is a palatial one, always it is pleasant and homelike. The hotels are not always as good as they might be, and the stranger who has access to the Club is grateful for his privilege and knows how to value it.

☆ ☆ ☆

Kinchinjunga's peak was but fitfully visible, but in the between times it was vividly clear against the sky – away up there in the blue dome more than 28,000 feet above sea level – the loftiest land I had ever seen, by 12,000 feet or more. It was 45 miles away. Mount Everest is a thousand feet higher, but it was not a part of that sea of mountains piled up there before me, so I did not see it; but I did not care, because I think that mountains that are as high as that are disagreeable.

☆ ☆ ☆

On Monday and Tuesday at sunrise we again had fair-to-middling views of the stupendous mountains; then, being well cooled off and refreshed, we were ready to chance the weather of the lower world once more.

We traveled up hill by the regular train five miles to the summit, then changed to a little canvas-canopied hand-car for the 35

way to see the country. JOHN PAUL DEJORIA

mile descent. It was the size of a sleigh, it had six seats and was so low that it seemed to rest on the ground. It had no engine or other propelling power, and needed none to help it fly down those steep inclines. It only needed a strong brake, to modify its flight, and it had that. There was a story of a disastrous trip made down the mountain once in this little car by the Lieutenant-Governor of Bengal, when the car jumped the track and threw its passengers over a precipice. It was not true, but the story had value for me, for it made me nervous, and nervousness wakes a person up and makes him alive and alert, and heightens the thrill of a new and doubtful experience. The car could really jump the track, of course; a pebble on the track, placed there by either accident or malice, at a sharp curve where one might strike it before the eye could discover it, could derail the car and fling it down into India; and the fact that the lieutenant-governor had escaped was no proof that I would have the same luck. And standing there, looking down upon the Indian Empire from the airy altitude of 7,000 feet, it seemed unpleasantly far, dangerously far, to be flung from a handcar.

But after all, there was but small danger – for me. What there was, was for Mr. Pugh, inspector of a division of the Indian police, in whose company and protection we had come from Calcutta. He had seen long service as an artillery officer, was less nervous than I was, and so he was to go ahead of us in a pilot hand-car, with a Ghurka and another native; and the plan was that when we should see his car jump over a precipice we must put on our (brake) and send for another pilot. It was a good arrangement. Also Mr. Barnard, chief engineer of the mountain-division of the road, was to take personal charge of our car, and he had been down the mountain in it many a time.

Everything looked safe. Indeed, there was but one questionable detail left: the regular train was to follow us as soon as we should start, and it might run over us. Privately, I thought it would.

The road fell sharply down in front of us and went corkscrewing in and out around the crags and precipices, down, down, forever down, suggesting nothing so exactly or so uncom-

Everyone needs three umbrellas – one to leave at the

fortably as a crooked toboggan slide with no end to it. Mr. Pugh waved his flag and started, like an arrow from a bow, and before I could get out of the car we were gone too. I had previously had but one sensation like the shock of that departure, and that was the gaspy shock that took my breath away the first time that I was discharged from the summit of a toboggan slide. But in both instances the sensation was pleasurable – intensely so; it was a sudden and immense exaltation, a mixed ecstasy of deadly fright and unimaginable joy. I believe that this combination makes the perfection of human delight.

The pilot car's flight down the mountain suggested the swoop of a swallow that is skimming the ground, so swiftly and smoothly and gracefully it swept down the long straight reaches and soared in and out of the bends and around the corners. We raced after it, and seemed to flash by the capes and crags with the speed of light; and now and then we almost overtook it – and had hopes; but it was only playing with us; when we got near, it released its brake, made a spring around a corner, and the next time it spun into view, a few seconds later, it looked as small as a wheelbarrow, it was so far away. We played with the train in the same way. We often got out to gather flowers or sit on a precipice and look at the scenery, then presently we would hear a dull and growing roar, and the long coils of the train would come into sight behind and above us; but we did not need to start till the locomotive was close down upon us – then we soon left it far behind. It had to stop at every station, therefore it was not an embarrassment to us. Our brake was a good piece of machinery; it could bring the car to a standstill on a slope as steep as a house-roof.

☆ ☆ ☆

A few miles down the mountain we stopped half an hour to see a Thibetan dramatic performance. It was in the open air on the hillside. The audience was composed of Thibetans, Ghurkas, and other unusual people. The costumes of the actors were in the last degree outlandish, and the performance was in keeping with the clothes. To an accompaniment of barbarous noises the actors stepped out one after another and began to spin around with

office, one to leave at home, and one to leave on the train.
Paul Dickson

immense swiftness and vigor and violence, chanting the while, and soon the whole troupe would be spinning and chanting and raising the dust. They were performing an ancient and celebrated historical play, and a Chinaman explained it to me in pidjin English as it went along. The play was obscure enough without the explanation; with the explanation added, it was opake. As a drama this ancient historical work of art was defective, I thought, but as a wild and barbarous spectacle the representation was beyond criticism. Far down the mountain we got out to look at a piece of remarkable loop-engineering – a spiral where the road curves upon itself with such abruptness that when the regular train came down and entered the loop, we stood over it and saw the locomotive disappear under our bridge, then in a few moments appear again, chasing its own tail; and we saw it gain on it, overtake it, draw ahead past the rear cars, and run a race with that end of the train. It was like a snake swallowing itself.

Half-way down the mountain we stopped about an hour at Mr. Barnard's house for refreshments, and while we were sitting on the veranda looking at the distant panorama of hills through a gap in the forest, we came very near seeing a leopard kill a calf. – [It killed it the day before.] – It is a wild place and lovely. From the woods all about came the songs of birds, – among them the contributions of a couple of birds which I was not then acquainted with: the brain-fever bird and the coppersmith. The song of the brain-fever demon starts on a low but steadily rising key, and is a spiral twist which augments in intensity and severity with each added spiral, growing sharper and sharper, and more and more painful, more and more agonizing, more and more maddening, intolerable, unendurable, as it bores deeper and deeper and deeper into the listener's brain, until at last the brain fever comes as a relief and the man dies. I am bringing some of these birds home to America. They will be a great curiosity there, and it is believed that in our climate they will multiply like rabbits.

☆ ☆ ☆

And so, presently we took to the hand-car and went flying down the mountain again; flying and stopping, flying and stop-

A good traveller has no fixed plans and

ping, till at last we were in the plain once more and stowed for Calcutta in the regular train. That was the most enjoyable day I have spent in the earth. For rousing, tingling, rapturous pleasure there is no holiday trip that approaches the bird-flight down the Himalayas in a hand-car. It has no fault, no blemish, no lack, except that there are only thirty-five miles of it instead of five hundred.

(From *Following the Equator*; American Publishing Co, 1898)

The Overland Mail: Foot-Service to the Hills, 1886

RUDYARD KIPLING

Even when the railways had come to India they had not brought the post to many of the towns and villages – still a runner had to carry them ....

In the name of the Empress of India, make way,
O Lords of the Jungle, wherever you roam,
The woods are astir at the close of the day –
We exiles are waiting for letters from Home.
Let the robber retreat – let the tiger turn tail –
In the name of the Empress, the Overland Mail!

With a jingle of bells as the dusk gathers in,
He turns to the footpath that heads up the hill –
The bags on his back and a cloth round his chin,
And tucked in his waistbelt, the Post Office bill: –
'Despatched on this date, as received by the rail,
'Per runner, two bags of the Overland Mail'.

Is the torrent in spate? He must ford it or swim.
Has the rain wrecked the road? He must climb by the cliff.
Does the tempest cry halt? What are tempests to him?
The service admits not a 'but' or an 'if'
While the breaths in his mouth, he must bear without fail,
In the name of the Empress, the Overland Mail.

From aloe to rose-oak, from rose-oak to fir,
From level to upland, from upland to crest,
From rice-field to rock-ridge, from rock-ridge to spur,
Fly the soft sandalled feet, strains the brawny brown chest.
From rail to ravine – to the peak from the vale –
Up, up through the night goes the Overland Mail.

There's a speck on the hillside, a dot on the road –
A jingle of bells on the footpath below –
There's a scuffle above in the monkey's abode –
The world is awake and the clouds are aglow.
But the great Sun himself must attend to the hail: –
'In the name of the Empress, the Overland Mail!'

(From *Departmental Ditties and Other Verses*; 1886)

Quest for Kim – 'Te-rain', 1996

PETER HOPKIRK

The author travelled around India by train following the journeys that Rudyard Kipling's famous young hero Kim made in the search for the 'Great Game' of the British Indian secret service. Hopkirk's adventures in his search almost match those of his hero … .

My first blow was the discovery, while still in London, that there is no longer a 5.25 a.m. night express from Lahore to Umballa. Although disappointing, I confess that this did not come as any great surprise. After all, if Kim was born in 1865, then we are talking about a rail journey made in 1878, well over a century ago. Of course, there may never have been a 5.25 a.m. train – something which could, no doubt, be verified from a contemporary timetable. However, Kipling, who never lost his reporter's eye for detail, was not given to investigating things unnecessarily. Moreover, he goes on to explain just why there was a train at so ungodly an hour.

'All hours are alike to Orientals,' he writes in *Kim*, 'and their passenger traffic is regulated accordingly.'

Furthermore, I was astonished to discover that another train

All travel has its advantages. If the passenger visits better carries him to worse, he may learn

which features in a later chapter of the novel does still run precisely at the same time today as it did then.

☆ ☆ ☆

The Thomas Cook overseas railway timetable, which I consulted in London and from which I had discovered that there was no longer a night train to Umballa, informed me instead that there was now a daily train departing at 11.30 a.m. As this was the sole train of the day, I thought it wise to double check, especially when I noticed that the author of the Lonely Planet guide book gave the departure time at 11 a.m. He added, as a cautionary note perhaps, that 'we have never used this train'.

The discovery that the train was now only twice weekly was annoying, since it gave me less flexibility when I got to Lahore.

☆ ☆ ☆

There can be few such bloodstained railway stations as that of Lahore, though the Pakistan Tourist Development Corporation may be forgiven for not drawing attention to its strategic but horrific past.

My thoughts were on anything but the past as I hurried into the station, for my sole concern at that moment was to find out once and for all about trains for Umballa. With bats circling overhead in the gloom, I first made for what Kim calls 'that hole' – the ticket office – where the clerk he informs the lama, 'will give thee a paper to take thee to Umballa.' Whether it is the same 'hole' as in Kim's day, where the young Kipling would have bought his tickets too, I doubt, as it looks far too new. But from this 'hole' I was politely directed to another, not far away, where I was told they would know when the trains left for Amritsar and Umballa. They did not, and I was again re-directed, this time to 'Upper Class Reservations', though I was determined, like Kim and the lama, to go third class. Once more I was politely shunted on, without even having discovered whether there were still trains to Umballa.

I now made my way, as instructed to 'Advance Reservations', which lay at the very end of one of the platforms. However, as I did so I spotted an impressive looking, uniformed figure, with an

countries, he may learn to improve his own. And if fortune to enjoy it. SAMUEL JOHNSON

equally impressive moustache, who appeared to be the station master, or possibly his deputy. I asked him if he could tell me when the trains left for Umballa. He looked at me in surprise, or perhaps it was out of pity, and then somewhat ominously suggested that I would do far better to take a taxi to Amritsar, and pick up the Indian train there for the onward journey to Umballa. It was obviously pointless my explaining why I had to go by train, as it was highly unlikely that he had even so much as heard of Kim, of which – or so one Lahore bookseller assured me – there has never been an Urdu translation.

Hopkirk eventually, after he had asked further helpful people, was told that the train was not allowed to stop at Umballa, even for a foreign passenger. However, he managed to find out that he could go by an indirect route and he decided to do just that.

(From *Quest for Kim: in Search of Kipling's Great Game;* John Murray, 1996,

Forbidden Train in Upper Burma, 1975

Paul Theroux

The author spent four months travelling across Asia by train, at first following the Hippy Trail to India and finally returning to Europe on the Trans-Siberian to produce his classic travelogue, 'The Great Railway Bazaar'. In Burma he attempts to take The Lashio Mail, through the jungle and over the Gokteik Viaduct to the border with China. He begins on the train from Mandalay to Maymyo...

Asia washes with spirited soapy violence in the morning. The early train takes you past people discovered laundering like felons rehearsing – Pakistanis charging their sodden clothes with sticks, Indians trying to break rocks (this is Mark Twain's definition of a Hindu) by slapping them with wet *dhotis*, grimacing Ceylonese wringing out their lungis. In Upper Burma, women squat in conspiratorial groups at bubbly streams, whacking their laundry flat with broad wooden paddles, children totter knee-deep in rock pools, and small-breasted girls, chastely covered by sarongs to their armpits, dump buckets of water over their heads.

It was dull and cloudy, starting to mist, as we left Mandalay, and the old man next to me with a neat cloth bundle on his knees watched one of these bathing girls.

☆ ☆ ☆

At the early sloping stations, women with trays were selling breakfast to the passengers: oranges, sliced pawpaws, fried cakes, peanuts, and bananas. One had a dark shining assortment of beady objects on her tray. I beckoned her over and had a look. They were fat insects skewered on sticks – fried locusts. I asked the old man next to me if he'd like some. He said politely that he had had breakfast already, and anyway he never ate insects. 'But the local people are quite fond of them.'

☆ ☆ ☆

'... Ah, this is Maymyo.' ... Bernard said, 'Where are you putting up?'

I said I didn't have the slightest idea. 'Then you should come to Candacraig,' he said. 'I am the manager – shall I book you in?'

'Yes,' I said. 'I'll be along later – I have to buy a ticket to Gokteik.'

Looking for the ticket office, I stumbled into the radio operator's room where a bearded Eurasian with a yellow cravat and slicked-down hair was seated, listening to Morse code and scribbling on a pad. He looked at me and jumped up, reaching for my hand. 'Is there anything I can do for you?' ...

I told him I wanted to take the train to Gokteik, but I had heard it was forbidden.

'No problem. When do you want to go? Tomorrow? There's a train at seven. Sure, I can get you on it. I suppose you want to see the bridge – it's a nice one. Funny, not many people come up here. About a year ago there was a chap – he was English – heading for Lashio. The soldiers stopped him and, put him off the train at Hsipaw. He was in a terrible shape – all disconnected. I told him not to worry. The police came and made a little trouble, but the next day I put him on the train to Lashio and when the police came at nine o'clock I said, 'He's in Lashio,' so there wasn't anything they could do.'

and remember more than I have seen. BENJAMIN DISRAELI

'Is it against the law to go to Gokteik?' 'Maybe yes, maybe no. No one knows – but I'll get you on the train. Don't worry.'

☆ ☆ ☆

Travellers to Lashio were converging on the station: a rattling procession of *tongas* and stagecoaches down the avenue of eucalyptus trees; women running with shopping bags, clenching cigars in their teeth, and men dressed as frontiersmen, in boots and black hats, dodging the plodding oxen, who pulled wagonloads of firewood (split and bright, the colour of torn flesh) in the opposite direction. I had left my camera and passport behind; I felt the legality of the trip to Gokteik was questionable and I wanted to appear as unsuspicious a traveller as possible.

Tony, the Eurasian, was waiting for me. He took my three kyats and got me a ticket to Naung-Peng, the station after Gokteik. There was nothing but a bridge at Gokteik, he said, but there was a good canteen at Naung-Peng. We walked down the muddy platform to the last car. Three soldiers in mismatched uniforms – the poor fit indicating they might have been looted in the dark from some tiny enemies – stood outside the car, passing chopped betel nut across the barrels of the rifles they carried loosely at their shoulders. Tony spoke in Burmese to the tallest one, who nodded meaningfully at me. It struck me that their dented helmets and hand-me-down uniforms gave them the grizzled, courageous look you see in embattled legionnaires – a kind of sloppiness that seemed indistinguishable from hard-won experience.

'You will be safe here,' said Tony. 'Ride in this carriage.'

Ten years of guerrilla war in the outlying states of Upper Burma, as well as the persistent depredations of dacoits who hold up trains with homemade guns, have meant that the last car on the train is traditionally reserved for a group of armed escorts. They sit in this car, their vintage Enfields thrown higgledy-piggledy on the wooden benches, their woollen ear-flaps swinging; they lounge, eating bananas, slicing betel nut, reddening the floor with spittle; and they hope for a shot at a rebel or a thief. I was told they seldom have any luck. The rebels are demoralized

Your true traveler finds boredom rather agreeable than
He accepts his boredom, when it comes, not merely

and don't show their faces; but the thieves, wise to the escorts in the last car, have learned to raid the first few cars quickly, threatening passengers noisily with daggers, and can be safely back in the jungle before the soldiers can run up the line.

Our departure whistle put the crows to flight, and we were off, bowling along the single track. The early morning fog had become fine mist, the mist drizzle, but not even the considerable amount of rain that poured through the windows persuaded any of the soldiers (eating, reading, playfully fighting) to close the shutters. The windows that admitted light admitted rain: you had to choose between that and a dry darkness on upcountry trains. I sat on the edge of my bench, regretting that I hadn't brought anything to read, wondering if it really was illegal for me to be travelling to the Gokteik Viaduct, and feeling pity for the children I saw in soaked clothes splashing through the cold puddles in their bare feet.

Then the train pulled into a siding and stopped. Up ahead was a station, a wooden shed the size of a two-car garage. Its window boxes held the orange and red blossoms the Burmese call 'Maymyo flowers'. Some men in the forward coaches got out to piss. Two small girls ran from the jungle next to the line to sell bananas from enamel basins on their heads. Ten minutes passed, and a man appeared at the window waving a piece of paper, a leaf from the kind of pad on which Tony had scribbled his Morse code messages. This paper was passed to the tall soldier with the Sten gun, who read it out loud in an announcing voice. The other soldiers listened intently; one turned, and, with a swiftness I took to be embarrassment, glanced at me. I got up and walked to the back of the carriage, but before I reached the exit the soldier studying the message – a man who had only smiled apologetically earlier when I asked him if he could speak English – said, 'Sit down please.' I sat down. A soldier muttered. The rain increased, making a boiling sputter on the roof.

The soldier put down his Sten gun and came over to me. He showed me the message. It was written in pencil, rows and rows of Burmese script that resembled the code in the Sherlock Holmes story 'The Adventure of the Dancing Men'. But in the middle of all the dancing men, those crooked heads and arms, those kicking legs, were two English words in capital letters: 'PASS BOOK'.

'You have pass book?'

'No pass book,' I said.

'Where you going?'

'Gokteik, Naung-Peng,' I said. 'Just for the ride. Who wants to know?'

He thought a moment; then folded the paper over and with the stub of a pencil wrote very carefully in a wobbly column, *Name*, *Number*, *Country*, and *Pass book*. He handed me the paper. I gave him the information, while the rest of the soldiers – there were six altogether – gathered around. One peered over my shoulder, sucked his teeth, and said 'American'. The others verified this, putting their heads close and breathing on to my hand.

The message was taken to the wooden shed. I stood up. One of the soldiers said, 'Sit down.'

Two hours passed, the coach dripped, the roof boiled in the downpour, and the soldiers who had been speaking in whispers, perhaps fearing that I knew Burmese, resumed their eating, shelling peanuts, peeling bananas, slicing betel nuts. I don't think time can pass more slowly than in a railway carriage parked in the rain between two low walls of jungle in Upper Burma. There was not even the diversion of hawkers, or the desperate antics of pariah dogs; there were no houses; the jungle was without texture or light; there was no landscape. I sat chilled to the bone watching raindrop rings widen in a pool of water next to the track, and I tried to imagine what had gone wrong. I had no doubt that I was the cause of the delay – there was an objection to my being on the train; I had been seen boarding in Maymyo. I would be sent back; or I might be arrested for violating security regulations, thrown into jail. The effort of getting so far seemed wasted; and, really, had I come all that way to find a jail, as people travel in the greatest discomfort to the farthest ends of the earth, through jungles and bad weather for weeks and weeks, to hurry into a doomed plane or step into the path of a bullet? It is ignominious when a person travels a great distance to die.

Tourists don't know where they've been, travellers

It wasn't death that worried me – they wouldn't be silly enough to kill me. But they could inconvenience me. Already; they had. It was past ten o'clock, and I was on the point of resigning. If the sun had been out I would have volunteered to walk back to Maymyo, turning the whole fiasco into a hike.

But it was raining too hard to do anything but sit and wait.

Finally the tall soldier with the Sten gun returned. He was accompanied by a small fellow, rather young, in a wet jacket and wet hat, who mopped his face with a handkerchief when he got inside the carriage. He said, 'You are Mister Paul?'

'Yes. Who are you?'

'Security Officer U Sit Aye,' he said, and went on to ask when I had entered Burma, and why, and for how long. Then he asked, 'You are a tourist?'

'Yes.'

He thought a moment, tilting his head, narrowing his hooded eyes, and said, 'Then where is your camera?'

'I left it behind,' I said. 'I ran out of film.'

'Yes, we have no film in Burma.' He sighed. 'No foreign exchange.'

As he spoke another train drew up beside the one we were in.

'We will get in that train.'

In the last armed coach of this second train, sitting with a new batch of soldiers, U Sit Aye said he was in charge of railway security; he had three children; he hated the rainy season. He said no more. I assumed he was my escort, and, though I had no idea why we had changed trains, we were on the move, travelling in the direction of Gokteik.

A haggard Burmese man in a woollen cap took a seat across from us and began emptying a filtertip cigarette on to a small square of paper. It was the sort of activity that occupied the foreign residents of Afghanistan hotels, a prelude to filling the empty tube with hashish grains and tobacco. But this man didn't have hashish. His drug, in a small phial, was white powder which he tapped into the tube, alternating it with layers of tobacco. He stuffed the tube with great care, packing it tight, smoothing and tapping it.

don't know where they're going. PAUL THEROUX

'What's he doing?'

'I do not know,' said U Sit Aye.

The man peered into his cigarette. It was nearly full; he poked it down with a match.

'He's putting something inside.'

'I can see,' said U Sit Aye.

'But it's not *ganja*.'

'No.'

Now the man was finished. He emptied the last of the powder and threw the phial out of the window.

I said, 'I think it's opium.'

The man looked up and grinned. 'You are right!'

His English, clear as a bell, startled me. U Sit Aye said nothing, and as he was not wearing a uniform the man had no way of knowing he was making an opium cigarette under the nose of a security officer.

'Have a puff,' said the man. He twisted the top and licked the whole cigarette so that it would burn slowly. He offered it to me.

'No thanks.'

He looked surprised. 'Why not?'

'Opium gives me a headache.'

'No! *Very* good! I like it –' He winked at U Sit Aye. '– I like it for nice daydreamings!' He smoked the cigarette to the filter, rolled up his jacket, and put it behind his head. He stretched out on the seat and went to sleep with a smile on his face. He was perfectly composed, the happiest man on that cold rattling train.

U Sit Aye said, 'We don't arrest them unless they have a lot. It's so much trouble. We put the chap in jail. We then send a sample to Rangoon for tests – but his is number three; I can tell by the colour – and after two or three weeks they send the report back. You need a lot of opium for the tests – enough for lots of experiments.'

Towards noon we were in the environs of Gokteik. The mist was heavy and noisy waterfalls splashed down through pipe thickets of green bamboo. We crawled around the upper edges of hills, hooting at each curve, but out the windows there was only the whiteness of mist, shifted by a strong wind to reveal the more intense whiteness of cloud. It was like travelling in a slow plane with the windows open, and I envied the opium smoker his repose.

'The views are clouded,' said U Sit Aye.

We climbed to nearly 4,000 feet and then began descending into the gorge where, below, boat-shaped wisps of cloud moved quickly across from hillside to hillside and other lengths of vapour depended in the gorge with only the barest motion, like veils of threadbare silk. The viaduct, a monster of silver geometry in all the ragged rock and jungle, came into view and then slipped behind an outcrop of rock. It appeared again at intervals, growing larger, less silver, more imposing. Its presence there was bizarre, this manmade thing in so remote a place, competing with the grandeur of the enormous gorge and yet seeming more grand than its surroundings, which were hardly negligible – the water rushing through the girder legs and falling on the tops of trees, the flights of birds through the swirling clouds and the blackness of the tunnels beyond the viaduct. We approached it slowly, stopping briefly at Gokteik Station, where hill people, tattooed Shans and straggling Chinese, had taken up residence in unused railway cars – freight cars and sheds. They came to the doors to watch the Lashio Mail go past.

There were wincing sentries at the entrance to the viaduct with rifles on their shoulders; the wind blew through their wall-less shelters and the drizzle continued. I asked U Sit Aye if I could hang out the window. He said it was all right with him, 'but don't fall.' The train wheels banged on the steel spans and the plunging water roared the birds out of their nests a thousand feet down. The long delay in the cold had depressed me, and the journey had been unremarkable, but this lifted my spirits, crossing the long bridge in the rain, from one steep hill to another; over a jungly deepness, bursting with a river to which the monsoon had given a hectoring voice, and the engine whistling again and again, the echo carrying down the gorge to China.

The tunnels began, and they were cavernous, smelling of bat shit and sodden plants, with just enough light to illuminate the water rushing down the walls and the odd night-blooming flowers growing amid fountains of creepers and leaves in the twisted stone. When we emerged from the last tunnel we were far from the Gokteik Viaduct, and Naung-Peng, an hour more of steady travelling, was the end of the line for me. This was a collection of wooden shacks and grass-roofed shelters. The 'canteen' Tony had told me about was one of these grass-roofed huts: inside was a long table with tureens of green and yellow stew, and Burmese, thinly clad for such a cold place, were warming themselves beside cauldrons of rice bubbling over braziers.

☆ ☆ ☆

The return to Maymyo, downhill most of the way, was quick, and there was a continuous intake of food at small stations. U Sit Aye explained that the soldiers wired ahead for the food, and it was true, for at the smallest station a boy would rush up to the train as soon as it drew in, and with a bow this child with rain on his face would present a parcel of food at the door of the soldiers' coach. Nearer to Maymyo they wired ahead for flowers, so when we arrived each soldier stepped out with curry stains on his shirt, a plug of betel in his mouth, and a bouquet of flowers, which he clutched with greater care than his rifle.

'Can I go now?' I said to U Sit Aye. I still didn't know whether I was going to be arrested for going through forbidden territory.

'You can go,' he said, and smiled. 'But you must not take the train to Gokteik again. If you do there will be trouble.'

(From *The Great Railway Bazaar*; Penguin, 1977, © Paul Theroux)

Up the Khyber Pass, 1993

Mark Tully

For his episode of the television documentary series, 'Great Rail Journeys', Mark Tully (former South Asia correspondent of the BBC) chose a classic rail journey in Pakistan covering the length of the country from Karachi to the Khyber Pass. The Khyber Mail runs from Karachi to Peshawar but the line up the Khyber Pass from there has been closed since the Russo-Afghan War. A steam special up the pass was, however, laid on for the film crew and this has also been used by tourists.

I often look lovingly at my 1910 *Bradshaw* and think of the days when trains really mattered in Britain. What makes Pakistan exciting is that they do still matter there. Neither cars nor aeroplanes have displaced them yet as the usual means of transport for a long journey. Almost anyone can travel, too – you don't have to have an expense account to afford a ticket. Stations are crowded, noisy places, where every arrival and departure is an occasion. The fact that the railways are still the mainstay of Pakistan's transport system gives passengers from countries meant to be more advanced the pleasurable impression that they have gone back in time. This impression is heightened by the stately progress trains make. Style has not been sacrificed for speed.

Passengers can sit in the doorway, watching the cows come home in the evening and enjoying the unmistakable smell of village suppers cooking on dung fires.

Mind you, many Pakistanis don't appreciate their old-fashioned railway system. One of the officials I met when negotiating filming permission said: 'I only have one objection. To make a 'positive' film about Pakistan Railways is a major disservice to the travelling public.' But then, making fun of the railways is just the survival of another tradition.

The Khyber Mail is, to me anyhow, the most romantic of all the trains which cross the subcontinent, yet in nearly twenty-five years living there I had never travelled on it. It runs the length of Pakistan, from Karachi near the mouth of the River Indus to Peshawar at the foot of the Khyber Pass, a distance of 1050 miles. It takes two nights and a day to complete its journey, travelling at an average speed of about 32 miles per hour, which of course includes some lengthy stops at stations. The Mail often travels even slower than its schedule and is frequently subject to what railwaymen in Pakistan call 'late running', but then punctuality is no more the essence of a Pakistani railway journey than speed. If a train is scheduled to go fast you expect it to do just that, and get tense and irritated when it's even a few minutes late. In South Asia you happily hand over your destiny to the railways, and set-

only who is foreign. ROBERT LOUIS STEVENSON

tle down to enjoy the luxury of being completely cut off from the rest of the world for the longer the better.

☆ ☆ ☆

[At Karachi Cantonment], the Station Superintendent took me to the signal box high above the platforms, where he showed me how ancient and modern survive side by side on Pakistan Railways. There was a device for controlling the latest colour light signalling, but one of the signalmen was laboriously plotting the progress of trains by drawing lines on a chart with a pencil and ruler. The station announcer alternately broadcast the impending arrival of the Sind Express and read out prayers for the safe departure of the next train. When the British Raj ended in 1947, Pakistan was divided from India to fulfil the demand for a Muslim homeland. Islam is therefore the be-all and end-all of the nation.

The Khyber Mail was shunted into the platform well before its departure time. The mail had to be loaded into the travelling post office, where it would be sorted throughout the night and dropped off at the appropriate stations. The passengers' heavy baggage had to be booked into the luggage brake. The conductors had to deal with the inevitable arguments about reservations. Bribes had to be offered and sometimes taken – demand exceeds supply, and so there is a black market in berths.

While these preparations for the journey were being made, red-shirted coolies were pouring through the platform gates balancing loads of luggage on their heads. Chai-wallahs noisily urged passengers to have one more cup of tea before departure. The crowd on the platform grew denser and denser as more and more people came to see off their friends or relatives; it is a very lonely and sad Pakistani who can't find anyone to come and say goodbye at the start of a long railway journey. Above all the hubbub, the station announcer still vainly tried to make his voice heard.

To the uninitiated it looked like a scene of sheer chaos. I knew it was the anarchy of the subcontinent, out of which order of a sort always miraculously emerges. Sure enough, just before ten o'clock a shrill whistle rose above the din of departure, and the guard waved his green lamp. At the far end of the platform, the fireman put his head inside the cab and said to the driver, 'Right away.' There was a raucous blast from the diesel locomotive, and the Khyber Mail started slowly on its long journey. Passengers who were still saying their farewells scrambled aboard, forcing their way into crowded economy-class carriages. As I stood in splendid isolation in the open doorway of my first-class compartment, watching the platform pass and seeing the guard still waving his green light, I was reminded of my excitement as a child when the train which took us on family holidays used to pull out of Calcutta's Howrah Station. 'Diesel may have replaced steam,' I thought, 'but thank God little else has changed.'

As the train gathered speed I was shown to my compartment by the sleeping car attendant. It was what is known in the subcontinent as a coupé – a two-berth cabin, air-conditioned and with its own lavatory and washbasin. The attendant was inordinately pleased when I told him that in India even first-class air-conditioned passengers don't get their own loo. He asked whether Pakistan Railways were better than Indian in other ways, too; I said I would let him know when I finished my journey. Pakistanis seem to need constant reassurance that they are doing better than India, whether that's true or not. The ill will created by partition has led to a bitter rivalry between the two countries.

☆ ☆ ☆

Although the railways have been perhaps the most lasting legacy of the British Raj, in 1844, when the first proposal to build a railway was put to the Directors of the East India Company, they were not convinced of its usefulness and suggested only limited experiments. Amongst the Directors' fears were 'the ravages of insects and vermin upon timber and earthwork'. A civil engineer thought that the surface of India was so uneven and overcrowded with cattle and goats that the lines would need to be suspended from chains at a height of at least eight feet above the ground. There were concerns about the commercial viability of

rather than miles. TIM CAHILL

the railways, too, although it's difficult to see how anyone could doubt they would overcome their main competition, the bullock cart. Then there were the potential passengers themselves, who were worried about making contact with people from other castes in crowded railway carriages, and wondered how they would find a train which started at an auspicious time. In the end commercial common sense, combined with defence needs, overcame all objections. Most of the North Western Railway consists of what were known as strategic lines – that is to say, lines where defence and not commerce was the reason for their construction.

☆ ☆ ☆

Lahore Station, like so many in the turbulent territory that the North Western Railway ran through, was built like a fort. When I congratulated the Superintendent, Mohammed Afzal, on his magnificent station he said, 'You built it. We haven't added a single brick since independence.' Then he went on with a smile, 'Of course, we may have taken one or two away.' He told me my train to Rawalpindi was a little late because the electric locomotive had broken down a few miles outside the station. Only about 175 miles of the main line have been electrified, and this means that most passengers are unaccustomed to the dangers of overhead wires. The railway timetable politely 'requests passengers in their own interests not to travel on footboards of trains; not to travel on the roofs of the carriages; and not to lean out of doors and windows of carriages' when trains are travelling on the electrified sector. According to the Station Superintendent, remarkably few do. He said only about one person a year got electrocuted by travelling on the roof.

The six-hour journey to Rawalpindi was eventful. We crushed a scooter at a level crossing. Fortunately the owner had run for it when he realized he couldn't get across before the train. Our next unscheduled halt was due to mechanical trouble. Because of shortage of foreign exchange the railways had over the years been forced to beg for engines from various aid donors. This had led to the acquisition of what Iqbal Samad described as a 'zoo of locomotives', each species having different spare parts, with all the difficulties that causes. Fortunately spare parts were no problem this time – a brick for a hammer and some string were all that the driver needed – and we were soon on our way.

☆ ☆ ☆

Pindi to Peshawar is the last stage of the Khyber Mail's journey. By this time many of the carriages have been shed, partly because there is not that much traffic on the sector, and partly because the loop lines where crossings take place are too short to take a full-length train. Speeds between Rawalpindi and Peshawar are slower, too. It takes the Khyber Mail four hours and five minutes to cover 108 miles – an average speed of just 27 miles per hour. That is partly because, although it's meant to be a long-distance train linking the main cities of Pakistan, the Khyber Mail stops at an inordinate number of small stations in the early hours of the morning as it completes the last stage of its run to Peshawar.

☆ ☆ ☆

In Peshawar there was no room at the old-fashioned Deans Hotel, so I had to stay at the modem Pearl Continental. There was a notice by the reception desk saying: 'Arms cannot be brought inside the hotel premises. Personal guards or gunmen are requested to deposit their weapons with the hotel security. We seek your cooperation – The Management.' I am sure the management does not always get that cooperation, because every man in the North West Frontier Province regards it as his right to carry a gun.

Preferring Pathan cooking to the Pearl Continental's, I went out that evening to the Medina mosque which is surrounded by small restaurants, with carcasses of goats hanging from butchers' hooks outside. The proprietors sit cross-legged, cutting meat with knives held between their toes. Their speciality is goat cooked in a *karhai*, which is somewhat similar to a Chinese wok. Tomatoes, chillies and *dhaniya* or coriander are added, and the meat is then cooked, I was told, 'until it speaks'. If it's a little tough, some water is added. My *karhai gosht* was beautifully tender, and I managed not to be put off my food by the basket under my table full of bones discarded by earlier diners.

what he has come to see. GK CHESTERTON

Peshawar should have been the end of my journey, because the line which runs on to the summit of the Khyber was officially closed during the Soviet-Afghan war – although one Englishman who lived in Peshawar in those days did tell me he had seen some ammunition trains being hauled up the pass. By great good fortune, however, Pakistan Railways had just decided to revive the line for tourists and they put on a preliminary train for our film.

Two steam engines, once again resplendent in their black livery and magnificently adorned, awaited me just the other side of Peshawar Airport. It was a push-me-pull-you train, with the engine at the front pointing towards the Khyber and the engine at the other end pointing back towards Peshawar. I was told that the engines had been built in 1913 and 1919 in Britain, but were still quite capable of making the long haul up the Khyber. The train consisted of a restaurant car, a parlour car, a generator and a brake van. We were the only passengers, but there was an army of railway employees to accompany us.

I climbed on to the footplate of the front engine and we edged slowly forward on a flat stretch of line running through the suburbs of Peshawar. I felt inordinately proud as we moved majestically through the crowds which had turned out to see the Khyber train running again. At a level crossing terrified tonga ponies reared in their shafts, shivering with fear, nostrils flaring; they had never seen snorting monsters like the steam engines which were bearing down on them.

We were soon in sight of the narrow V in the rampart of mountains ahead which marked the entrance of the Khyber. The inspector who had travelled with me from Jacobabad to Sibi was on the footplate again. He rechecked all the gauges and had a hurried word with the driver to make sure we were fully prepared for the long climb. Then we lumbered through the entrance to the Khyber and were engulfed by the pass. The beat of the pistons grew longer and longer and echoed off the barren yellow mountains. Mechanics sat on the front of the engine waiting to pounce on any fault which might develop. I looked back as we rounded yet another corner and saw the Pakistan flags fluttering proudly below the boiler of the back engine. The smoke from its funnel left a dark patch in the bright, clear, sunlit air. Then we plunged into one of the thirty-four tunnels. Smoke filled my eyes and the roar of not one but two engines deafened me. I could well imagine how the Amir of Afghanistan, a land without trains, got so alarmed when passing through the longest tunnel on the North Western that he pulled the communication cord.

Eventually we ground to a halt at the first of the zigzags, where the gradient is so steep that the train has to reverse to climb it. Pathan tribesmen, all armed, appeared from nowhere to watch the train change direction, and the rear engine become the front one. Above us we could see the second zigzag, where the original order would be restored. We had some difficulty in getting away from the second change of direction: there were anxious consultations on the telephone connected to the engine at the back. It was essential that the rear engine should get the train moving before we opened our regulator, otherwise we would pull the train apart. After much huffing and hooting I felt the train move forward slightly, our driver let steam into the cylinders and we resumed our slow but steady progress until we reached the grim, high-walled Shagai fort. There we stopped to take water.

☆ ☆ ☆

Even the innovative engineers who had built the Bolan line considered the Khyber to be impassable by rail, but after the Third Afghan War in 1919 it was decided that an effort would have to be made. British troops were now posted at the summit of the Khyber, and they needed a railway to supply them. One of the first jobs was to persuade the Pathan tribal leaders to accept a railway running through their territory. They were totally opposed to it until Victor Bayley, the engineer who was to build the railway, told them that the trains would be very slow and therefore easy to loot. After that the Pathans even agreed to be the contractors.

It was dangerous terrain to work in, and the support of the tribal leaders was always uncertain. The British political agent warned Bayley, 'Whether it's the climate or the underlying strain under which we all live, a man cracks up suddenly if he goes on too long. It's no place for weaklings.' An army officer told him to be very careful of the Pathans, saying, 'They are pretty poisonous blighters.' Bayley himself found them 'murderous ruffians', but then went on to say that they were not much different from contractors anywhere else in the world.

The conditions under which Bayley had to work were not easy, either. Much of the material had to be carried up the mountainside by donkeys so hardy that when a lorry ran into a pack of them they all survived. In high winds the surveyors' theodolites blew over, and in the extreme heat a haze made the sightings waver. But Bayley persevered, and after five years trains ran to the Afghan border – making India, in his view,'impregnable for the cost of a single battleship'.

Our train steamed slowly into Landi Kotal, the summit of the Khyber and the end of the line. The track which ran from there down the mountains to the Afghan border below had been taken up before the British left. The entire population of the small town, renowned for its smugglers and its handicraft – arms manufacturing – seemed to be on the platform. The station itself is a two-storeyed fort built of stone and surrounded by a high wall, behind which the staff live. The only access to the public is a small booking office window which can double as a machine-gun loop.

I was taken through the grim gates in the high wall to the courtyard to meet the staff and have my last cup of tea with Pakistan Railways. Then I went to say farewell to the train. The two engines stood against the background of the brown mountains. Smoke curled from their funnels as they rested from their great labour. Their green Pakistan flags fluttered proudly. It was evening. Hauling tourists is far less gallant than holding the Khyber Pass, but only holidaymakers can now prevent night falling over that unique railway and its proud engines.

(From *Great Rail Journeys*; Penguin, 1995, © Mark Tully)

Travel is glamorous only in retrospect.
PAUL THEROUX

NORTH AMERICA

Canadian Railways, 1907

KARL BAEDEKER

In 1907 railways were still 'news' and many people wanted to know where they went, how they worked, what they cost, and what it was like to travel on them. Baedeker satisfied much of their interest – in a way that would be surprising in any book on railways today ….

The Dominion of Canada now contains about 20,000 miles of railway, or about one-tenth less than the United Kingdom. Fully two thirds of the entire amount are in the hands of the Canadian Pacific Railway (8298 miles in 1905), the Grand Trunk Railway (3111 miles), the Canadian Northern System (1880 miles), and the Government (1419 miles). The capital invested in railways amounted in 1905 to about $248,666,000, of which about 20% had been contributed by state and municipal aid. In the same year the railways carried 25,288,723 passengers and 50,893,957 tons of freight. The total receipts were $106,467,199, showing a surplus of about 25 per cent over operating costs.

The standard gauge (4 foot 8½ inches) is in use by almost all the railways of Canada.

The equipments of the Canadian Railways are similar to those of the United States lines, which, as is well known, are very different from those of European railways. Instead of comparatively small coaches, divided into compartments holding 6-8 people each, the American railways have long cars (like an enlarged tramway car), holding 60-70 persons, entered by doors at each end, and having a longitudinal passage down the middle, with the seats on each side of it. Each seat has room for two passengers. All long distance trains are furnished with drawing room (parlour) cars, and are in every way much more comfortable.

(From *The Dominion of Canada with Newfoundland and an excursion to Alaska*; Karl Baedeker, 1907)

An American Railroad, 1842

Charles Dickens

Dickens visited America in 1842 and was treated like a celebrity, with a grand ball given in his honour in New York on St Valentine's Day. His enthusiasm for America waned, however, as the trip progressed. He was unimpressed by what he saw of the politics ('This is not the republic of my imagination.' he wrote). But most of all he was annoyed to find that with no international copyright laws at the time, Americans could read his books in much cheaper editions, denying him significant earnings.

I made acquaintance with an American railroad, on this occasion, for the first time. As these works are pretty much alike all through the States, their general characteristics are easily described.

There are no first and second class carriages as with us; but there is a gentleman's car and a ladies' car: the main distinction between which is that in the first, everybody smokes; and in the second, nobody does. As a black man never travels with a white one, there is also a negro car; which is a great, blundering, clumsy chest, such as Gulliver put to sea in, from the kingdom of Brobdingnag. There is a great deal of jolting, a great deal of noise, a great deal of wall, not much window, a locomotive engine, a shriek, and a bell.

The cars are like shabby omnibuses, but larger: holding thirty, forty, fifty, people. The seats, instead of stretching from end to end, are placed crosswise. Each seat holds two persons. There is a long row of them on each side of the caravan, a narrow passage up the middle, and a door at both ends. In the centre of the carriage there is usually a stove, fed with charcoal or anthracite coal; which is for the most part red-hot. It is insufferably close; and you see the hot air fluttering between yourself and any other object you may happen to look at, like the ghost of smoke.

One always begins to forgive a place as

In the ladies' car, there are a great many gentlemen who have ladies with them. There are also a great many ladies who have nobody with them: for any lady may travel alone, from one end of the United States to the other, and be certain of the most courteous and considerate treatment everywhere. The conductor or check-taker, or guard, or whatever he may be, wears no uniform. He walks up and down the car, and in and out of it, as his fancy dictates; leans against the door with his hands in his pockets and stares at you, if you chance to be a stranger; or enters into conversation with the passengers about him. A great many newspapers are pulled out, and a few of them are read. Everybody talks to you, or to anybody else who hits his fancy. If you are an Englishman, he expects that that railroad is pretty much like an English railroad. If you say 'No,' he says 'Yes?' (interrogatively), and asks in what respect they differ. You enumerate the heads of difference, one by one, and he says 'Yes?' (still interrogatively) to each. Then he guesses that you don't travel faster in England; and on your replying that you do, says 'Yes?' again (still interrogatively), and it is quite evident, don't believe it. After a long pause he remarks, partly to you, and partly to the knob on the top of his stick, that 'Yankees are reckoned to be considerable of a go-ahead people too,' upon which YOU say 'Yes,' and then HE says 'Yes' again (affirmatively this time); and upon your looking out of window, tells you that behind that hill, and some three miles from the next station, there is a clever town in a smart lo-ca-tion, where he expects you have concluded to stop. Your answer in the negative naturally leads to more questions in reference to your intended route (always pronounced rout); and wherever you are going, you invariably learn that you can't get there without immense difficulty and danger, and that all the great sights are somewhere else.

If a lady take a fancy to any male passenger's seat, the gentleman who accompanies her gives him notice of the fact, and he immediately vacates it with great politeness. Politics are much discussed, so are banks, so is cotton. Quiet people avoid the question of the Presidency, for there will be a new election in three

soon as it's left behind. CHARLES DICKENS

years and a half, and party feeling runs very high: the great constitutional feature of this institution being, that directly the acrimony of the last election is over, the acrimony of the next one begins; which is an unspeakable comfort to all strong politicians and true lovers of their country: that is to say, to ninety-nine men and boys out of every ninety-nine and a quarter.

Except when a branch road joins the main one, there is seldom more than one track of rails; so that the road is very narrow, and the view, where there is a deep cutting, by no means extensive. When there is not, the character of the scenery is always the same. Mile after mile of stunted trees: some hewn down by the axe, some blown down by the wind, some half fallen and resting on their neighbours, many mere logs half hidden in the swamp, others mouldered away to spongy chips. The very soil of the earth is made up of minute fragments such as these; each pool of stagnant water has its crust of vegetable rottenness; on every side there are the boughs, and trunks, and stumps of trees, in every possible stage of decay, decomposition, and neglect. Now you emerge for a few brief minutes on an open country, glittering with some bright lake or pool, broad as many an English river, but so small here that it scarcely has a name; now catch hasty glimpses of a distant town, with its clean white houses and their cool piazzas, its prim New England church and school-house; when whir-r-r-r! almost before you have seen them, comes the same dark screen: the stunted trees, the stumps, the logs, the stagnant water — all so like the last that you seem to have been transported back again by magic.

The train calls at stations in the woods, where the wild impossibility of anybody having the smallest reason to get out, is only to be equalled by the apparently desperate hopelessness of there being anybody to get in. It rushes across the turnpike road, where there is no gate, no policeman, no signal: nothing but a rough wooden arch, on which is painted 'WHEN THE BELL RINGS, LOOK OUT FOR THE LOCOMOTIVE.' On it whirls headlong, dives through the woods again, emerges in the light, clatters over frail arches, rumbles upon the heavy ground, shoots beneath a wooden bridge which intercepts the light for a second

Black people lived right by the railroad tracks, and the train and I thought: I'm gonna make a song

like a wink, suddenly awakens all the slumbering echoes in the main street of a large town, and dashes on haphazard, pell-mell, neck-or-nothing, down the middle of the road. There — with mechanics working at their trades, and people leaning from their doors and windows, and boys flying kites and playing marbles, and men smoking, and women talking, and children crawling, and pigs burrowing, and unaccustomed horses plunging and rearing, close to the very rails — there — on, on, on — tears the mad dragon of an engine with its train of cars; scattering in all directions a shower of burning sparks from its wood fire; screeching, hissing, yelling, panting; until at last the thirsty monster stops beneath a covered way to drink, the people cluster round, and you have time to breathe again.

(From *American Notes for General Circulation;* Chapman & Hall, 1842)

Aboard the Immigrant Train, 1879

ROBERT LOUIS STEVENSON

Born in Scotland in 1850, Stevenson studied law at Edinburgh University. As well as being a novelist (best known for 'Treasure Island' and 'Kidnapped'), he was also a poet and prolific travel writer. In France he met and fell in love with Fanny Osbourne, an American 10 years older than him and already married. Three years later she cabled from California for him to come to her. Stevenson's parents were against the liaison and, with very little money, he decided to travel to America as an Immigrant. Special Immigrant Trains were laid on to meet the Immigrant Boats which sailed from Europe to the East Coast. Stevenson published an account of the trip: 'Across the Plains'.

At a place called Creston, a drunken man got in. He was aggressively friendly, but, according to English notions, not at all unpresentable upon a train. For one stage he eluded the notice of the officials; but just as we were beginning to move out of the next station, Cromwell by name, by came the conductor. There was a word or two of talk; and then the official had the man by the shoulders, twitched him from his seat, marched him through the

would shake their houses at night. I would hear it as a boy, that sounds like that. LITTLE RICHARD

car, and sent him flying on to the track. It was done in three motions, as exact as a piece of drill.

The train was still moving slowly, although beginning to mend her pace, and the drunkard got his feet without a fall. He carried a red bundle, though not so red as his cheeks; and he shook this menacingly in the air with one hand, while the other stole behind him to the region of the kidneys. It was the first indication that I had come among revolvers, and I observed it with some emotion. The conductor stood on the steps with one hand on his hip, looking back at him; and perhaps this attitude imposed upon the creature, for he turned without further ado, and went off staggering along the track towards Cromwell, followed by a peal of laughter from the cars. They were speaking English all about me, but I knew I was in a foreign land.

☆ ☆ ☆

It was about two in the afternoon of Friday that I found myself in front of the Emigrant House, with more than a hundred others, to be sorted and boxed for the journey. A white-haired official, with a stick under one arm, and a list in the other hand, stood apart in front of us, and called name after name in the tone of a command. At each name you would see a family gather up its brats and bundles and run for the hindmost of the three cars that stood awaiting us, and I soon concluded that this was to be set apart for the women and children. The second or central car, it turned out, was devoted to men travelling alone, and the third to the Chinese.

I suppose the reader has some notion of an American railroad-car, that long, narrow wooden box, like a flat-roofed Noah's ark, with a stove and a convenience, one at either end, a passage down the middle, and transverse benches upon either hand.

Those destined for emigrants on the Union Pacific are only remarkable for their extreme plainness, nothing but wood entering in any part into their constitution, and for the usual inefficacy of the lamps, which often went out and shed but a dying glimmer even while they burned.

The benches are too short for anything but a young child.

I travel not to go anywhere, but to go. I travel

Where there is scarce elbow-room for two to sit, there will not be space enough for one to lie. Hence the company, or rather, as it appears from certain bills about the Transfer Station, the company's servants, have conceived a plan for the better accommodation of travellers. They prevail on every two to chum together. To each of the chums they sell a board and three square cushions stuffed with straw, and covered with thin cotton.

The benches can be made to face each other in pairs, for the backs are reversible. On the approach of night the boards are laid from bench to bench, making a couch wide enough for two, and long enough for a man of the middle height; and the chums lie down side by side upon the cushions with the head to the conductor's van and the feet to the engine. When the train is full, of course this plan is impossible, for there must not be more than one to every bench, neither can it be carried out unless the chums agree.

☆ ☆ ☆

A great personage on an American train is the newsboy. He sells books (such books !), papers, fruit, lollipops, and cigars; and on emigrant journeys, soap, towels, tin washing-dishes, tin coffee pitchers, coffee, tea, sugar, and tinned eatables, mostly hash or beans and bacon.

Early next morning the newsboy went around the cars, and chumming on a more extended principle became the order of the hour. It requires but a co-partnery of two to manage beds; but washing and eating can be carried on most economically by a syndicate of three. I myself entered a little after sunrise into articles of agreement, and became one of the firm of Pennsylvania, Shakespeare, and Dubuque.

Shakespeare was my own nickname on the cars; Pennsylvania that of my bedfellow; and Dubuque, the name of a place in the State of Iowa, that of an amiable young fellow going west to cure an asthma, and retarding his recovery by incessantly chewing or smoking, and sometimes chewing and smoking together. I have never seen tobacco so sillily abused.

Shakespeare bought a tin washing-dish, Dubuque a towel,

for travel's sake. The great affair is to move.
ROBERT LOUIS STEVENSON

and Pennsylvania a brick of soap. The partners used these instruments, one after another, according to the order of their first awaking; and when the firm had finished there was no want of borrowers. Each filled the tin dish at the water filter opposite the stove, and retired with the whole stock in trade to the platform of the car. There he knelt down, supporting himself by a shoulder against the woodwork; or one elbow crooked about the railing, and made a shift to wash his face and neck and hands-a cold, an insufficient, and, if the train is moving rapidly, a somewhat dangerous toilet.

(From *Across the Plains*; Chatto & Windus, 1915)

The Iron Horse, 1891

EMILY DICKINSON

I like to see it lap the miles,
And lick the valleys up,
And stop to feed itself at tanks;
And then, prodigious, step

Around a pile of mountains,
And, supercilious, peer
In shanties by the sides of roads;
And then a quarry pare

To fit its sides, and crawl between,
Complaining all the while
In horrid, hooting stanza;
Then chase itself down the hill

And neigh like Boanerges;
Then, punctual as a star,
Stop – docile and omnipotent –
At its own stable door.

(From *The Poems of Emily Dickinson*; 1891)

A private railroad car is not an acquired taste.

Special Train across America, 1896

RUDYARD KIPLING

Harvey Cheyne Jnr is the 15-year-old son of the rail magnate of the same name, who is washed overboard from a transatlantic steamship. Having assumed that he has drowned, his parents have just learnt that he has been rescued off the Grand Banks of Newfoundland. Cheyne Snr uses his influence to organise a special train to rush across America to his son.

So the truth was told. Miss Kinzey clicked in the sentiment while the secretary added the memorable quotation, 'Let us have peace,' and in board rooms two thousand miles away the representatives of sixty-three million dollars' worth of variously manipulated railroad interests breathed more freely. Cheyne was flying to meet the only son, so miraculously restored to him. The bear was seeking his cub, not the bulls. Hard men who had their knives drawn to fight for their financial lives put away the weapons and wished him God-speed, while half a dozen panic-smitten tin-pot toads perked up their heads and spoke of the wonderful things they would have done had not Cheyne buried the hatchet.

It was a busy week-end among the wires; for now that their anxiety was removed, men and cities hastened to accommodate. Los Angeles called to San Diego and Barstow that the Southern California engineers might know and be ready in their lonely roundhouses; Barstow passed the word to the Atlantic and Pacific; and Albuquerque flung it the whole length of the Atchinson, Topeka, and Santa Fe management, even into Chicago. An engine, combination-car with crew, and the great and gilded 'Constance' private car were to be 'expedited' over those two thousand three hundred and fifty miles. The train would take precedence of one hundred and seventy-seven others meeting and passing; despatchers and crews of every one of those said trains must be notified. Sixteen locomotives, sixteen engineers, and sixteen firemen would be needed – each and every one the best available. Two and one half minutes would be allowed for changing engines, three for watering, and two for coaling. 'Warn the men, and arrange tanks and chutes accordingly; for Harvey Cheyne is in a hurry, a hurry, a hurry,' sang the wires. 'Forty miles an hour will be expected, and division superintendents will accompany this special over their respective divisions. From San Diego to Sixteenth Street, Chicago, let the magic carpet be laid down. Hurry! Oh, hurry!'

'It will be hot,' said Cheyne, as they rolled out of San Diego in the dawn of Sunday. 'We're going to hurry, Mama, just as fast as ever we can; but I really don't think there's any good of your putting on your bonnet and gloves yet. You'd much better lie down and take your medicine. I'd play you a game of dominoes, but it's Sunday.'

'I'll be good. Oh, I will be good. Only – taking off my bonnet makes me feel as if we'd never get there.'

'Try to sleep a little, Mama, and we'll be in Chicago before you know.'

'But it's Boston, Father. Tell them to hurry.'

The six-foot drivers were hammering their way to San Bernardino and the Mohave wastes, but this was no grade for speed. That would come later. The heat of the desert followed the heat of the hills as they turned east to the Needles and the Colorado River. The car cracked in the utter drouth and glare, and they put crushed ice to Mrs. Cheyne's neck, and toiled up the long, long grades, past Ash Fork, towards Flagstaff, where the forests and quarries are, under the dry, remote skies. The needle of the speed-indicator flicked and wagged to and fro; the cinders rattled on the roof, and a whirl of dust sucked after the whirling wheels. The crew of the combination sat on their bunks, panting in their shirtsleeves, and Cheyne found himself among them shouting old, old stories of the railroad that every trainman knows, above the roar of the car. He told them about his son, and how the sea had given up its dead, and they nodded and spat and rejoiced with him; asked after 'her, back there,' and whether she could stand it if the engineer 'let her out a piece,' and Cheyne thought she could. Accordingly, the great

Neither a wise man nor a brave man lies down on the

fire-horse was 'let out' from Flagstaff to Winslow, till a division superintendent protested.

But Mrs. Cheyne, in the boudoir stateroom, where the French maid, sallow-white with fear, clung to the silver door-handle, only moaned a little and begged her husband to bid them 'hurry.' And so they dropped the dry sands and moon-struck rocks of Arizona behind them, and grilled on till the crash of the couplings and the wheeze of the brake-hose told them they were at Coolidge by the Continental Divide.

Three bold and experienced men – cool, confident, and dry when they began; white, quivering, and wet when they finished their trick at those terrible wheels – swung her over the great lift from Albuquerque to Glorietta and beyond Springer, up and up to the Raton Tunnel on the State line, whence they dropped rocking into La Junta, had sight of the Arkansaw, and tore down the long slope to Dodge City, where Cheyne took comfort once again from setting his watch an hour ahead.

There was very little talk in the car. The secretary and typewriter sat together on the stamped Spanish-leather cushions by the plate-glass observation-window at the rear end, watching the surge and ripple of the ties crowded back behind them, and, it is believed, making notes of the scenery. Cheyne moved nervously between his own extravagant gorgeousness and the naked necessity of the combination, an unlit cigar in his teeth, till the pitying crews forgot that he was their tribal enemy, and did their best to entertain him.

At night the bunched electrics lit up that distressful palace of all the luxuries, and they fared sumptuously, swinging on through the emptiness of abject desolation.

Now they heard the swish of a water-tank, and the guttural voice of a Chinaman, the click-clink of hammers that tested the Krupp steel wheels, and the oath of a tramp chased off the rear-platform; now the solid crash of coal shot into the tender; and now a beating back of noises as they flew past a waiting train. Now they looked out into great abysses, a trestle purring beneath their tread, or up to rocks that barred out half the stars. Now

tracks of history to wait for the train of the future to run over him. DWIGHT D. EISENHOWER

scour and ravine changed and rolled back to jagged mountains on the horizon's edge, and now broke into hills lower and lower, till at last came the true plains.

At Dodge City an unknown hand threw in a copy of a Kansas paper containing some sort of an interview with Harvey, who had evidently fallen in with an enterprising reporter, telegraphed on from Boston. The joyful journalese revealed that it was beyond question their boy, and it soothed Mrs. Cheyne for a while. Her one word 'hurry' was conveyed by the crews to the engineers at Nickerson, Topeka, and Marceline, where the grades are easy, and they brushed the Continent behind them. Towns and villages were close together now, and a man could feel here that he moved among people.

'I can't see the dial, and my eyes ache so. What are we doing?'

'The very best we can, Mama. There's no sense in getting in before the Limited. We'd only have to wait.'

'I don't care. I want to feel we're moving. Sit down and tell me the miles.'

Cheyne sat down and read the dial for her (there were some miles which stand for records to this day), but the seventy-foot car never changed its long steamer-like roll, moving through the heat with the hum of a giant bee. Yet the speed was not enough for Mrs. Cheyne; and the heat, the remorseless August heat, was making her giddy; the clock-hands would not move, and when, oh, when would they be in Chicago?

It is not true that, as they changed engines at Fort Madison, Cheyne passed over to the Amalgamated Brotherhood of Locomotive Engineers an endowment sufficient to enable them to fight him and his fellows on equal terms for evermore. He paid his obligations to engineers and firemen as he believed they deserved, and only his bank knows what he gave the crews who had sympathized with him. It is on record that the last crew took entire charge of switching operations at Sixteenth Street, because 'she' was in a doze at last, and Heaven was to help any one who bumped her.

Now the highly paid specialist who conveys the Lake Shore and Michigan Southern Limited from Chicago to Elkhart is some-

I'm proud to be a rail modeller. It means more to me to be

thing of an autocrat, and he does not approve of being told how to back up to a car. None the less he handled the 'Constance' as if she might have been a load of dynamite, and when the crew rebuked him, they did it in whispers and dumb show.

'Pshaw!' said the Atchinson, Topeka, and Santa Fe men, discussing life later, 'we weren't runnin' for a record. Harvey Cheyne's wife, she were sick back, an' we didn't want to jounce her. Come to think of it, our runnin' time from San Diego to Chicago was 57.54. You can tell that to them Eastern way-trains. When we're tryin' for a record, we'll let you know.'

To the Western man (though this would not please either city) Chicago and Boston are cheek by jowl, and some railroads encourage the delusion. The Limited whirled the 'Constance' into Buffalo and the arms of the New York Central and Hudson River (illustrious magnates with white whiskers and gold charms on their watch-chains boarded her here to talk a little business to Cheyne), who slid her gracefully into Albany, where the Boston and Albany completed the run from tide-water to tide-water – total time, eighty-seven hours and thirty-five minutes, or three days, fifteen hours and one half. Harvey was waiting for them.

(From *Captains Courageous. A Story of the Grand Banks*; 1896)

on the cover of *Model Railroader* than to be on the cover of a music magazine. ROD STEWART

5 FURTHER AFIELD

Cairo to the Convent of Sinai, 1878

Karl Baedeker

Baedeker's German guidebooks covered many countries popular with 19th-century tourists and with their precise attention to detail were soon translated into English.

Cairo to Suez by rail:

Ayun Musa is 6 hours and 20 minutes. Ain Hawârah is 16½ hours. Wadi Useit is 2 hours and 15 minutes. Wadi et-Taiyibeh is 4 hours.

Total journey is 31 hours and 5 minutes.

Cairo to Suez – The railway being now open, most travellers will prefer sending forward their camels and escort and taking the train. At present (1874) there is but one train in the day. It leaves Cairo at 9am, reaches Zigazig about 12.30, Ismailîyeh at 4pm, and Suez at 7.30. The whole distance is only 150 miles, and might as easily be got over in half the time.

Those who wish to survey the intervening country may do so. The distance direct is, for camels, 32 hours.

(From *Egypt, Part I: Lower Egypt with the Fayum and the Peninsula of Sinai*; Karl Baedeker, 1878)

On an African Train, 1949

Rosemary Wells

For her book, 'A Gentle Pioneer', Rosemary Wells followed in the footsteps of her grandmother, Nancye Stuart, one of the original pioneers who trekked north from South Africa into the country that was then Southern Rhodesia. For the first part of the trip she took the train.

From the dusty windows of the old train I could see the vast expanse of beautiful valleys and miles of trees and vines overflowing with their ripening fruits – and over all the true blue sky stretching for ever towards the endless horizon, broken at intervals with grape-purple hills. Africa! I was here, in Africa, at last. After nearly twenty years of longing I was in the country of my dreams. Ever since, as a small child in England, I had listened to my mother's stories of her home in the bush, I knew this was a journey I would take one day.

But since leaving Cape Town, we had only reached the northern border of South Africa – and now, once across the 'great, grey-green, greasy Limpopo River' we changed into what my mother would call a 'real train', run on steam. The carriages, painted in the distinctive cream and purplish red of Rhodesian Railways, patiently awaited and welcomed their passengers – no commuter rush and bustle here. Once we were all comfortably settled in our leather-bound compartments, the gleaming old engine, with its highly polished brasses, huffed and puffed as its wheels began to turn and no-one seemed to mind the flecks of coal dust blowing into the windows as it began its slow, but comfortable journey towards Southern Rhodesia.

Outside the earth was dry, cracking in places following a summer of drought, and red dust swirled as we chugged past. And as I savoured the warmth of the air, smelled the smoke from the ashes of local fires, and tasted the roughness of dust on my tongue, I felt I was home at last. Suddenly I saw clumps of the tall, stately, smooth-barked eucalyptus trees, gum trees as we called them, every one of which I loyally believed to have been planted by my grandfather. Amongst them surprisingly green acacias gave shade to small clusters of mud huts, thatch-roofed, from which small children would run and wave at our slowly-passing train. More exciting to me was the sight of the occasional baobab tree – that curious tree around which so many ancient myths survive, and that the Africans call the upside down tree on account of its branches resembling roots – which gives no shade.

Every few miles huge granite boulders balanced awkwardly one on the other at angles that would baffle an engineer. 'They're our balancing rocks' a fellow passenger explained. For so long I

The first condition of understanding a foreign country is to smell it. Rudyard Kipling had felt I knew all there was to know about this vast, warm country, but I soon realized I had a lot to learn.

The first time the old train shuddered to a halt, several small boys chattering and smiling clambered on board trying to sell us their little bush babies – perhaps the smallest, certainly the most endearing of Africa's furry primates, with their huge eyes and long tails.

Now and then we would have glimpses of the straight asphalt road leading alongside our tracks, mesmerising for drivers in the midday sun in spite of little traffic. I thought of the days of my grandmother's first journey north. 'No roads then,' she had told me, 'just a few old tracks, used by hunters and trading wagons.'

(From *A Gentle Pioneer: Nancye Stuart*; Trailblazer, 2011, © Rosemary Wells)

To Lake Titicaca, 1983

Christopher Portway

The most evocative railways in South America are, surely, those of the trans-Andine lines. Two connect Chile and Argentina; three give landlocked Bolivia access to the Pacific, one links Lima with the mountain valleys and mineral region of central Peru, and the most northerly connects Guayaquil and Quito in Ecuador. These railways were built between 1870 and 1914, to a variety of gauges: standard gauge in Peru and metre gauge in Bolivia, and 3'6" gauge in Ecuador. At the time of their construction they helped to bring some political unity to the scattered and diverse population of the countries they served but their main function was economic and their chief interest freight traffic. They were, and still are, vitally important to the mining industries of Peru, Bolivia and Chile. Passenger traffic has never been more than a troublesome obligation.

Crossing the Andes meant constructing the highest railway in the world. The highest of all is the Peruvian Central Railway which I was to ride during my stay in that country. Railway construction in such circumstances presented civil engineers with major problems for they had, in a confined space and short dis-

The highest railway in the South America is in Peru where it also the world record but the Qinghai–Tibet Railway

tance, to build railways over passes which exceeded Mont Blanc in altitude. The solutions they adopted were tight curves, zigzags and rack sections. Operating the lines created further difficulties: steep gradients, lack of local sources of fuel, heavy wear and tear on locomotives and rolling stock and frequent landslides and washouts. Changing from steam to diesel was, initially, a step backwards because diesel units were prone to losing power in the rare air and there were many cases of trains being unable to take the gradients.

My first experience of riding a trans-Andine railway was on the Southern Railway of Peru. Three lines serve the *altiplano*, a grassy windswept plain 12,800 feet above sea level, and one of them is the Southern. Of standard gauge, it runs from Mollendo on the Peruvian coast through the country's second city, Arequipa, to the town of Juliaca on the *altiplano*. Here it divides. A short section continues to Lake Titicaca and around its shores to the port of Puno while a 211-mile line from Juliaca runs north to Cuzco – the ancient Inca capital, crossing a summit of 14,154 feet at La Raya. I planned to ride both. Access to Bolivia is maintained by a steamer service between Puno and the Bolivian port of Guaqui, and another short railway line to link with the capital, La Paz. The Southern Railway of Peru is not a major trans-Andine route but is, nevertheless, a very worthwhile ride. The line is single track throughout, and on the Arequipa to Mollendo section, the passenger trains have succumbed to road competition. This necessitated my having to travel from Lima to Arequipa by an overcrowded, smelly abomination of a bus that was delayed four hours during the intense heat of the midday sun by a nationwide bicycle race.

The city is full of old Spanish buildings and churches made of *sillar*, a pearly white volcanic material used almost exclusively for the construction of Arequipa. Though an Inca city it differs in many ways from Cuzco with few buildings taller than one storey. Earthquakes are the scourge here, the last being in 1960 when much damage was done. Travelling on a tight budget I knew my urban nights would have to be spent in the most basic of accommodations and the pension-cum-dosshouse I located at Arequipa set the standard.

reaches 4817m (15,803ft) at La Cima. Until 2006 this was in China now reaches 5068m (16,627ft) at Tanggula.

The Puno train was supposed to leave at 0815 and, in the event, left at 0915 which is not bad at all in a land where *mañana* doesn't just mean 'tomorrow' but can also mean 'never'. It was impressed upon me that tickets had to be purchased two hours in advance but there were no problems when I rolled up at the station ten minutes before the scheduled time of departure.

The early morning scene as the train wound up the valley towards Juliaca was enchanting. All around were fields of alfalfa and corn and, behind Arequipa, the volcanic peaks of Misti and Chachani. After Crucero Alto, the highest point on the line, the first mountain lakes appeared: Laguunillas and Saracocha, each on either side of the train. My guide book, ever practical, told me that all water east of Crucero Alta flowed into the Atlantic thousands of miles away.

I was travelling second – lowest – class and though the seats were hard my journey was not uncomfortable. The coaches were British-made, sturdy and ancient, their windows either jammed shut or jammed open. The train was full, but not overcrowded, with cheerful people. I was soon to learn that there is no need to go short of food on an Andean train ride for there are vendors both on the trains and at every stop. And Andean trains do a lot of stopping. All sorts of edible oddities were thrust under my nose by large peasant women wearing bowler hats and voluminous skirts of many colours inflated by layers of petticoats. There was no restaurant car on my train but that a kitchen existed was plain from the huge roast chicken dishes that none-too-clean waiters brought round to those that ordered them. With the chicken went generous measures of *Pisco* brandy which kept everyone in high spirits.

Except for some girls who, to my pleasurable but uncomprehending surprise, all bore a remarkable resemblance to Sophia Loren, my fellow travellers were of Indian extraction. The older womenfolk in their absurd hats and skirts wore their hair in standard greasy black plaits joined together at the nape of the neck. For most of the day-long journey everyone gorged themselves silly on huge chunks of semi-raw meat cut from an obscure joint of an equally obscure animal which was hawked by vendors

Travelling is like flirting with life. It's like saying, 'I would

from bundles of filthy rags. I stuck to the *Pisco* which possibly accounted for my being on a coach so liberally inhabited by Sophia Lorens. The train was diesel-hauled but so much black smoke issued from the locomotive it could have been a steam engine at our head.

Descending to fertile pampa I saw my first llama, alpaca or vicuna – I don't know which because the bowler-hatted brigade were each telling me something different, interspersed with great guffaws of laughter and display of nicotine-stained teeth. Juliaca, the junction, involved an interminable delay before the shores of Lake Titicaca came into sight and were slavishly followed by the train for the 30 miles to Puno. Weighed down by a heavy ruck-sack I fought my way off the seething platform.

(From *The Great Railway Adventure*; Coronet, 1985, © Christopher Portway)

Through the jungle in Brazil, 1994

Lisa St Aubin de Terán

For her episode of the television documentary series, 'Great Rail Journeys', novelist and poet Lisa St Aubin de Terán travelled 2000 miles from the Atlantic Ocean across Brazil and into Bolivia: from Santos to Santa Cruz.

Cut through the vegetation there are vast, stone-lined gullies, built by the British to drain away the torrential rains from the rails. It is hard to steal a moment from the scenery to pay homage to the daring engineering, the vision and the sacrifices required to build this line. I begin to be governed by hearsay, stopping off at places that have been recommended to me along the line. This is an anglophile stretch, all built by the British, who have left a trail of memorabilia behind them. In 1848, they built a winding gear to haul trains up the steep incline from Santos to Paranapiacaba, which means the place from which you can see the sea – as I am assured one can before eleven o'clock in the morning. After that, it is swallowed by a mist so dense that the station buildings seem to hover over the edge of the world; to venture beyond is an act of faith. The railways brought work, mobility, stability, the first

stay and love you but I have to go; this is my station'.
Lisa St Auban de Terán

cinema, football and a simplified version of cricket, so anything to do with trains is regarded with affection. Children in bright T-shirts and cotton shorts stand by to wave as the train arrives.

Paranapiacaba shrouded in mist has a moody, mysterious feel like being in a time warp: its meticulously-built brick hangars are immense and surreal. In one, a collection of antique carriages is preserved. There is the Emperor Pedro II's private compartment crowned with blue glass (glass, shutters, tombstones, houses, lorries and even weeds seem to be blue here in Brazil). There is a British locomotive from 1907 and a funeral car from the same year, with a place for the coffin at one end and rows of wicker chairs for the mourners at the other. The cheerful directions of a group of railway workers gave no indication of this ghostly desolation. I feel like a grave-robber violating a tomb. I grew up next to the Transport Museum in London, paying court to state carriages and famous engines that were all cordoned off from the public and out of bounds. These ones are open to the corrosive touch of mist and men alike, but the voracious local midges are a plague and they prevent me from prying any longer.

I return, via the tracks, stepping over the slippery, eroded hardwood sleepers. I ask when the next train to Sao Paulo arrives and am greeted by toothless amusement. This is still the first stretch of my projected two thousand or so miles, and it is one of the shortest legs, so I find it slightly unnerving that all attempts to establish a timetable are met with either diametrically contrasting answers or hilarity. I find I have so much time that I may as well be a moving target to the midges, and return to the railway remains to see the hauling gear which is the pride of Paranapiacaba. To get there entails crossing the equivalent of the paupers' cemetery, past burnt out and abandoned trains rusting into their tracks.

Then a train whistles into the station, apparently unexpectedly, and I have a job to catch it.

(From *Great Rail Journeys*; Penguin, 1995, © Lisa St Aubin de Terán)

The steepest railway in the world is the Katoomba
The gradient is 1 in 0.82 and

Sydney to Melbourne by Rail, 1895

Mark Twain

Owing to a failed investment in a new kind of typesetting machine in the early 1890s, Mark Twain was virtually bankrupt. As a means to earn money he embarked on a lecture tour of the British Empire in 1895 visiting India, Australia, New Zealand and South Africa. After his talks in Sydney he took the train to Melbourne.

So we moved south with a westward slant, 17 hours by rail to the capital of the colony of Victoria, Melbourne – that juvenile city of sixty years, and half a million inhabitants. On the map the distance looked small; but that is a trouble with all divisions of distance in such a vast country as Australia. The colony of Victoria itself looks small on the map – looks like a county, in fact – yet it is about as large as England, Scotland, and Wales combined. Or, to get another focus upon it, it is just 80 times as large as the state of Rhode Island, and one-third as large as the State of Texas.

Outside of Melbourne, Victoria seems to be owned by a handful of squatters, each with a Rhode Island for a sheep farm. That is the impression which one gathers from common talk, yet the wool industry of Victoria is by no means so great as that of New South Wales. The climate of Victoria is favorable to other great industries – among others, wheat-growing and the making of wine.

We took the train at Sydney at about four in the afternoon. It was American in one way, for we had a most rational sleeping car; also the car was clean and fine and new – nothing about it to suggest the rolling stock of the continent of Europe. But our baggage was weighed, and extra weight charged for. That was continental. Continental and troublesome. Any detail of railroading that is not troublesome cannot honorably be described as continental.

The tickets were round-trip ones – to Melbourne, and clear to Adelaide in South Australia, and then all the way back to Sydney. Twelve hundred more miles than we really expected to make; but then as the round trip wouldn't cost much more than the single trip, it seemed well enough to buy as many miles as one could afford, even if one was not likely to need them. A human being

Scenic Railway in the Blue Mountains, Australia.
the line is 310m (1020ft) long.

has a natural desire to have more of a good thing than he needs.

Now comes a singular thing: the oddest thing, the strangest thing, the most baffling and unaccountable marvel that Australasia can show. At the frontier between New South Wales and Victoria our multitude of passengers were routed out of their snug beds by lantern-light in the morning in the biting-cold of a high altitude to change cars on a road that has no break in it from Sydney to Melbourne! Think of the paralysis of intellect that gave that idea birth; imagine the boulder it emerged from on some petrified legislator's shoulders.

It is a narrow-gauge road to the frontier, and a broader gauge thence to Melbourne. The two governments were the builders of the road and are the owners of it. One or two reasons are given for this curious state of things. One is, that it represents the jealousy existing between the colonies – the two most important colonies of Australasia. What the other one is, I have forgotten. But it is of no consequence. It could be but another effort to explain the inexplicable.

All passengers fret at the double-gauge; all shippers of freight must of course fret at it; unnecessary expense, delay, and annoyance are imposed upon everybody concerned, and no one is benefitted.

Each Australian colony fences itself off from its neighbor with a custom-house. Personally, I have no objection, but it must be a good deal of inconvenience to the people. We have something resembling it here and there in America, but it goes by another name. The large empire of the Pacific coast requires a world of iron machinery, and could manufacture it economically on the spot if the imposts on foreign iron were removed. But they are not. Protection to Pennsylvania and Alabama forbids it. The result to the Pacific coast is the same as if there were several rows of custom-fences between the coast and the East. Iron carted across the American continent at luxurious railway rates would be valuable enough to be coined when it arrived.

We changed cars. This was at Albury. And it was there, I think, that the growing day and the early sun exposed the distant range called the Blue Mountains. Accurately named. 'My word!'

The longest stretch of straight railway track in the world straight track cross

as the Australians say, but it was a stunning color, that blue. Deep, strong, rich, exquisite; towering and majestic masses of blue – a softly luminous blue, a smouldering blue, as if vaguely lit by fires within. It extinguished the blue of the sky – made it pallid and unwholesome, whitey and washed-out. A wonderful color – just divine.

A resident told me that those were not mountains; he said they were rabbit-piles. And explained that long exposure and the over-ripe condition of the rabbits was what made them look so blue. This man may have been right, but much reading of books of travel has made me distrustful of gratis information furnished by unofficial residents of a country. The facts which such people give to travelers are usually erroneous, and often intemperately so. The rabbit-plague has indeed been very bad in Australia, and it could account for one mountain, but not for a mountain range, it seems to me. It is too large an order.

We breakfasted at the station. A good breakfast, except the coffee; and cheap. The Government establishes the prices and placards them. The waiters were men, I think; but that is not usual in Australasia. The usual thing is to have girls. No, not girls, young ladies – generally duchesses. Dress? They would attract attention at any royal levee in Europe. Even empresses and queens do not dress as they do. Not that they could not afford it, perhaps, but they would not know how.

All the pleasant morning we slid smoothly along over the plains, through thin – not thick – forests of great melancholy gum trees, with trunks rugged with curled sheets of flaking bark – erysipelas convalescents, so to speak, shedding their dead skins. And all along were tiny cabins, built sometimes of wood, sometimes of gray-blue corrugated iron; and the doorsteps and fences were clogged with children – rugged little simply-clad chaps that looked as if they had been imported from the banks of the Mississippi without breaking bulk.

And there were little villages, with neat stations well placarded with showy advertisements – mainly of almost too self-righteous brands of 'sheepdip.' If that is the name – and I think it is. It is a stuff like tar, and is dabbed on to places where the shear-

is in Western Australia where 478km (297 miles) of dead
the Nullarbor Plain.

er clips a piece out of the sheep. It bars out the flies, and has healing properties, and a nip to it which makes the sheep skip like the cattle on a thousand hills. It is not good to eat. That is, it is not good to eat except when mixed with railroad coffee. It improves railroad coffee. Without it railroad coffee is too vague. But with it, it is quite assertive and enthusiastic. By itself, railroad coffee is too passive; but sheep-dip makes it wake up and get down to business. I wonder where they get railroad coffee?

(From *Following the Equator;* American Publishing Co, 1898)

Railways in Australia, 1895

Mark Twain

En route to Maryborough he meets a man with strong views on the way the railways are run in Australia.

He had a good face, and a friendly look, and I judged from his dress that he was a dissenting minister. He was along toward fifty. Of his own motion he struck a match, and shaded it with his hand for me to light my cigar. I take the rest from my diary:

In order to start conversation I asked him something about Maryborough. He said, in a most pleasant – even musical voice, but with quiet and cultured decision:

'It's a charming town, with a hell of a hotel.'

I was astonished. It seemed so odd to hear a minister swear out loud. He went placidly on:

'It's the worst hotel in Australia. Well, one may go further, and say in Australasia.'

'Bad beds?'

'No – none at all. Just sand-bags.'

Having listed all the very many othe shortcomings of the hotel, he moved on to the railways ...

'...The government chooses to do its railway business in its own way, and it doesn't know as much about it as the French. In the beginning they tried idiots; then they imported the French – which was going backwards, you see; now it runs the roads itself – which is going backwards again, you see. Why, do you know, in order to curry favor with the voters, the government puts down a road wherever anybody wants it – anybody that owns two sheep and a dog; and by consequence we've got, in the colony of Victoria, 800 railway stations, and the business done at eighty of them doesn't foot up twenty shillings a week.'

'Five dollars? Oh, come!'

'It's true. It's the absolute truth.'

'Why, there are three or four men on wages at every station.'

'I know it. And the station-business doesn't pay for the sheep-dip to sanctify their coffee with. It's just as I say. And accommodating? Why, if you shake a rag the train will stop in the midst of the wilderness to pick you up. All that kind of politics costs, you see. And then, besides, any town that has a good many votes and wants a fine station, gets it. Don't you overlook that Maryborough station, if you take an interest in governmental curiosities. Why, you can put the whole population of Maryborough into it, and give them a sofa apiece, and have room for more. You haven't fifteen stations in America that are as big, and you probably haven't five that are half as fine. Why, it's perfectly elegant. And the clock! Everybody will show you the clock. There isn't a station in Europe that's got such a clock. It doesn't strike – and that's one mercy. It hasn't any bell; and as you'll have cause to remember, if you keep your reason, all Australia is simply bedamned with bells.

On every quarter-hour, night and day, they jingle a tiresome chime of half a dozen notes – all the clocks in town at once, all the clocks in Australasia at once, and all the very same notes; first, downward scale: mi, re, do, sol – then upward scale: sol, si, re, do – down again: mi, re, do, sol – up again: sol, si, re, do – then the clock – say at midnight clang – clang – clang – clang – clang – clang – clang – clang – clang – clang – – and, by that time you're – hello, what's all this excitement about? Oh I see – a runaway – scared by the train; why, you wouldn't think this train could scare anything. Well, of course, when they build and run eighty stations at a loss and a lot of palace-stations and clocks like Maryborough's at another loss, the government has got to economize somewhere hasn't it? Very well look at the rolling stock.

That's where they save the money. Why, that train from Maryborough will consist of eighteen freight-cars and two passenger-kennels; cheap, poor, shabby, slovenly; no drinking water, no sanitary arrangements, every imaginable inconvenience; and slow? – oh, the gait of cold molasses; no air-brake, no springs, and they'll jolt your head off every time they start or stop. That's where they make their little economies, you see. They spend tons of money to house you palatially while you wait fifteen minutes for a train, then degrade you to six hours' convict-transportation to get the foolish outlay back. What a rational man really needs is discomfort while he's waiting, then his journey in a nice train would be a grateful change. But no, that would be common sense – and out of place in a government. And then, besides, they save in that other little detail, you know – repudiate their own tickets, and collect a poor little illegitimate extra shilling out of you for that twelve miles, and – – '

'Well, in any case – – '

'Wait – there's more. Leave that American out of the account and see what would happen. There's nobody on hand to examine your ticket when you arrive. But the conductor will come and examine it when the train is ready to start. It is too late to buy your extra ticket now; the train can't wait, and won't. You must climb out.'

'But can't I pay the conductor?'

'No, he is not authorized to receive the money, and he won't. You must climb out. There's no other way. I tell you, the railway management is about the only thoroughly European thing here – continentally European I mean, not English. It's the continental business in perfection; down fine. Oh, yes, even to the peanut-commerce of weighing baggage.'

The train slowed up at his place. As he stepped out he said:

'Yes, you'll like Maryborough. Plenty of intelligence there. It's a charming place – with a hell of a hotel.'

Then he was gone. I turned to the other gentleman:

'Is your friend in the ministry?'

'No – studying for it.'

(From *Following the Equator*; American Publishing Co, 1898)

For me, the best places to write

The Indian Pacific to Perth, 2000

BILL BRYSON

Returning to Australia to make the country the subject of the eighth of his entertaining yet informative travelogues, Bryson writes: 'This is a country that is at once staggeringly empty and yet packed with stuff. Interesting stuff, ancient stuff, stuff not readily explained. Stuff yet to be found. Trust me, this is an interesting place.'

And so, in the company of the photographer Trevor Ray Hart, an amiable young man in shorts and a faded T-shirt, I took a cab to Sydney's Central Station, an imposing heap of bricks on Elizabeth Street, and there we found our way through its dim and venerable concourse to our train.

Stretching for a third of a mile along the curving platform, the Indian Pacific was everything the brochure illustrations had promised – silvery sleek, shiny as a new nickel humming with that sense of impending adventure that comes with the start of a long journey on a powerful machine. Carriage G, one of seventeen on the train, was in the charge of a cheerful steward named Terry, who thoughtfully provided a measure of local colour by accompanying every remark with an upbeat Aussie turn of phrase.

Need a glass of water?

'No worries, mate. I'll get right on 'er'.

Just received word that your mother has died?

'Not a drama. She'll be apples'.

He showed us to our berths, a pair of singles on opposite sides of a narrow panelled corridor. The cabins were astoundingly tiny – so tiny that you could bend over and actually get stuck.

'This is it?' I said in mild consternation. 'In its entirety?' 'No worries'. Terry beamed. 'She's a bit snug, but you'll find she's got everything you need.'

And he was right. Everything you could possibly require in a living space was there. It was just very compact, not much larger than a standard wardrobe. But it was a marvel of ergonomics. It included a comfy built-in seat, a hideaway basin and toilet, a

are on planes and trains. JO NESBO

miniature cupboard, an overhead shelf just large enough for one very small suitcase, two reading lights, a pair of clean towels and a little amenity bag. In the wall was a narrow drop-down bed, which didn't so much drop down as fall out like a hastily stowed corpse as I, and I expect many other giddily experimental passengers, discovered after looking ruminatively at the door and thinking: 'Well, I wonder what's behind *there*?' Still, it did make for an interesting surprise, and freeing my various facial protuberances from its coiled springs helped to pass the half hour before departure.

And then at last the train thrummed to life and we slid regally out of Sydney Central. We were on our way.

Done in one fell swoop, the journey to Perth takes nearly three days. Our instructions, however, were to disembark at the old mining town of Broken Hill to sample the outback and see what might bite us. So for Trevor and me the rail journey would be in two parts: an overnight run to Broken Hill and then a two-day haul across the Nullarbor. The train trundled out through the endless western suburbs of Sydney – through Flemington, Auburn, Parramatta, Doonside and the adorably named Rooty Hill – then picked up a little speed as we entered the Blue Mountains, where the houses thinned out and we were treated to long end-of-afternoon views over steep-sided vales and hazy forests of gum trees, whose quiet respirations give the hills their eponymous tinge.

I went off to explore the train. Our domain, the first class section, consisted of five sleeping carriages, a dining carriage in a plush and velvety style that might be called *fin de siècle brothel keeper*, and a lounge bar in a rather more modern mode. This was provisioned with soft chairs, a small promising-looking bar and low but relentless piped music from a twenty-volume compilation called, at a guess, 'Songs You Hoped You'd Never Hear Again'. A mournful duet from *Phantom of the Opera* was playing as I passed through.

Beyond first class was the slightly cheaper holiday class, which was much the same as ours except that their dining area was a buffet car with bare plastic tables. (These people apparent-

Boston's freeway system is insane. It was clearly designed

ly needed wiping down after meals.) The passage beyond holiday class was barred by a windowless door, which was locked.

What's back there?' I asked the buffet car girl.

'Coach class'. she said with a shudder.

'Is this door always locked?'

She nodded gravely. 'Always.'

Coach class would become my obsession. But first it was time for dinner. The tannoy announced the first sitting. Ethel Merman was belting out 'There's No Business Like Show Business' as I passed back through the first class lounge. Say what you will, the woman had lungs.

For all its air of cultivated venerability, the Indian Pacific is actually an infant as rail systems go, having been created as recently as 1970 when a new standard-gauge line was built across the country. Before that, for various arcane reasons mostly to do with regional distrust and envy, Australian railway lines employed different gauges. New South Wales had rails 4 feet 8½ inches apart. Victoria opted for a more commodious 5 feet 3 inches. Queensland and Western Australia economically decided on a standard of 3 feet 6 inches (a width not far off that of amusement park rides people must have ridden with their legs out of the windows). South Australia, inventively, had all three. Five times on any journey between the east and west coasts passengers and freight had to be offloaded from one train and redeposited on another; a mad and tedious process. Finally sanity was mustered and an all-new line was built. It is the second longest line in the word after Russia's Trans-Siberian.

(From *Down Under*; Black Swan, 2000, © Bill Bryson)

The Pleasure of Rail Travel, 2000

BILL BRYSON

The following morning we caught the second of the twice-weekly Indian Pacifics to Perth. In the deliciously air-chilled bar car of the train, Trevor and I spread out a map of Australia and discovered with astonishment that for all our hours of driving

by a person who had spent his childhood crashing toy trains.
BILL BRYSON

over the previous days we had covered only the tiniest fraction of land surface – a freckle, almost literally, on the face of Australia. It is such an immense country, and we still had 3,227 kilometres of it to get through before we reached Perth. There was nothing to do but sit back and enjoy it.

After the heat and dust of the outback, I was glad to be back in the clean, regulated world of the train, and I fell into its gentle routines with gratitude and relish. Train life, I decided, takes some beating. At some point in the morning, generally when you have gone for breakfast, your bed vanishes magically into the wall, and in the evening just as magically reappears, crisply made with fresh sheets. Three times a day you are called to the dining car, where you are presented with a thoroughly commendable meal by friendly and obliging staff. In between times there is nothing to do but sit and read, watch the endlessly unfurling scenery or chat with your neighbour. Trevor, because he was young and full of life and unaccountably had failed to bring any of my books to make the hours fly, felt restless and cooped up, but I wallowed in every undemanding minute of it.

With all your needs attended to and no real decisions to make, you soon find yourself wholly absorbed with the few tiny matters that are actually at your discretion – whether to have your morning shower now or in a while, whether to get up from your chair and pour yourself another complimentary cup of tea or be a devil and have a bottle of Victoria Bitter, whether to stroll back to your cabin for the book you forgot or just sit and watch the landscape for emus and kangaroos. If this sounds like a living death, don't be misled. I was having the time of my life. There is something wonderfully lulling about being stuck for a long spell on a train. It was like being given a preview of what it will be like to be in your eighties. All those things eighty-year-olds appear to enjoy – staring vacantly out of windows, dozing in a chair, boring the pants off anyone foolish enough to sit beside them – took on a special treasured meaning for me. This was the life!

(From *Down Under*; Black Swan, 2000, © Bill Bryson)

I never travel without my diary. One should always have something sensational to read on the train. OSCAR WILDE

BIBLIOGRAPHY

Auden, WH *Night Mail* (GPO Film Unit, 1936)
Baedeker, Karl *Egypt, Part I: Lower Egypt with the Fayum and the Peninsula of Sinai* (Karl Baedeker, 1878); *Great Britain: Handbook for Travellers* (Karl Baedeker, 1890); *Italy, Part 3: Southern Italy and Sicily, with Excursions into the Liparia Islands, Malta, Sardinia, Tunis, and Corfu* (Karl Baedeker, 1903); *Paris and environs, with routes from London to Paris* (Karl Baedeker, 1907); *The Dominion of Canada with Newfoundland and an excursion to Alaska* (Karl Baedeker, 1907)
Belloc, Hilaire *The Path to Rome* (Longmans, Green & Co, 1902)
Bennett, Arnold *How to Live on Twenty-Four Hours a Day* (1910)
Betjeman, John *High and Low* (John Murray, 1966), *John Betjeman Collected Poems* (John Murray, 2006)
Blanch, Lesley *Journey into the Mind's Eye* (Century, 1987)
Bryson, Bill *Down Under* (Black Swan, 2000)
Carroll, Lewis *Through the Looking-Glass* (1871)
Conan Doyle, Arthur *Tales of Terror and Mystery* (1923)
De La Mare, Walter *Songs of Childhood* (under pen name Walter Ramal, Longman, 1902)
Dickens, Charles *American Notes for General Circulation* (Chapman & Hall, 1842), *The Uncommercial Traveller* (1860)
Dickinson, Emily *The Poems of Emily Dickinson* (1891)
Eliot, George *Middlemarch* (1874)
Eliot, TS *Old Possum's Book of Practical Cats* (Faber & Faber, 1939)
Flanders & Swann *At the Drop of Another Hat* (1963)
Fleming, Peter *One's Company* (Cape, 1936)
Grahame, Kenneth *The Wind in the Willows* (Methuen, 1908)
Hardy, Thomas *A Laodicean: A Story of To-day, XII* (1881), *The Fiddler of the Reels* (Scribner's Magazine, 1893), *Selected Poems of Thomas Hardy* (Macmillan, 1916)
Hopkirk, Peter *Quest for Kim: in Search of Kipling's Great Game* (John Murray, 1996)
Kipling, Rudyard *Departmental Ditties and Other Verses* (1886), *Captains Courageous. A Story of the Grand Banks* (1896)
Larkin, Philip *The Collected Poems* (Faber & Faber, 1993)
Lomax, Eric *The Railway Man* (Vintage, 1996)
Maconie, Stuart *Pies and Prejudice* (Ebury Press, 2007)
McGonagall, William *Poetic Gems* (1890)
Meakin, Annette *A Ribbon of Iron* (Constable, 1901)
Nesbit, E *The Railway Children* (Wells, Gardner, Darton, 1906)
Newby, Eric *The Big Red Train Ride* (Penguin, 1980)
Owen, Wilfred *Poems* (1920)
Portway, Christopher *The Great Railway Adventure* (Coronet, 1985)
Railway News – Obituary of Thomas Cook, 1808-92 *Railway News* (23rd July 1892)

Rolt, LTC *Victorian Engineering: A fascinating story of invention and achievement* (Penguin, 1970)
Sassoon, Siegfried *The Old Huntsman and Other Poems* (EP Dutton, 1918)
St Aubin de Terán, Lisa *Great Rail Journeys* (Penguin, 1995)
Stevenson, Robert Louis *A Child's Garden of Verses* (1885), *Across the Plains* (Chatto & Windus, 1915)
Thackeray, William Makepeace *Roundabout Papers, De Juventute* (1863), *The Works of William Makepeace Thackeray* (Harper & Bros, 1899)
Theroux, Paul *The Great Railway Bazaar* (Penguin, 1977)
Thomas, Edward *Collected Poems* (Faber & Faber, 1920)
Thubron, Colin *In Siberia* (Penguin, 2000)
Trollope, Anthony *Orley Farm* (1862), *The Prime Minister* (1876)
Tully, Mark *Great Rail Journeys* (Penguin, 1995)
Twain, Mark *Following the Equator* (American Publishing Co, 1898)
Wells, Rosemary *A Gentle Pioneer: Nancye Stuart 1871-1956* (Trailblazer, 2011)

TRAILBLAZER TITLE LIST

A Gentle Pioneer: Nancye Stuart 1871-1956 (Biography)
Adventure Cycle-Touring Handbook
Adventure Motorcycling Handbook
Australia by Rail
Azerbaijan
Coast to Coast (British Walking Guide)

Cornwall Coast Path (British Walking Guide)
Corsica Trekking – GR20
Cotswold Way (British Walking Guide)
Dolomites Trekking – AV1 & AV2
Dorset & Sth Devon Coast Path (British Walking Gde)
Exmoor & Nth Devon Coast Path (British Walking Gde)
Hadrian's Wall Path (British Walking Guide)
Himalaya by Bike – a route and planning guide
Inca Trail, Cusco & Machu Picchu
Japan by Rail

Kilimanjaro – the trekking guide (includes Mt Meru)
Mediterranean Handbook
Morocco Overland (4WD/motorcycle/mountainbike)
Moroccan Atlas – The Trekking Guide
Nepal Trekking & The Great Himalaya Trail
New Zealand – The Great Walks
North Downs Way (British Walking Guide)
Norway's Arctic Highway
Offa's Dyke Path (British Walking Guide)

Overlanders' Handbook – worldwide driving guide
Peddars Way & Norfolk Coast Path (British Walking Gde)
Pembrokeshire Coast Path (British Walking Guide)
Pennine Way (British Walking Guide)
The Ridgeway (British Walking Guide)
Siberian BAM Guide – rail, rivers & road
The Silk Roads – a route and planning guide
Sahara Overland – a route and planning guide
Scottish Highlands – The Hillwalking Guide

Sinai – the trekking guide
South Downs Way (British Walking Guide)
Thames Path (British Walking Guide – due mid 2015)
Tour du Mont Blanc
Trans-Canada Rail Guide
Trans-Siberian Handbook
Trekking in the Everest Region
Trekking in Ladakh
The Walker's Anthology
The Walker's Haute Route – Mont Blanc to Matterhorn
West Highland Way (British Walking Guide)

For more information about Trailblazer and our expanding range of guides, for guidebook updates or for credit card mail order sales visit our website:

www.trailblazer-guides.com

INDEX

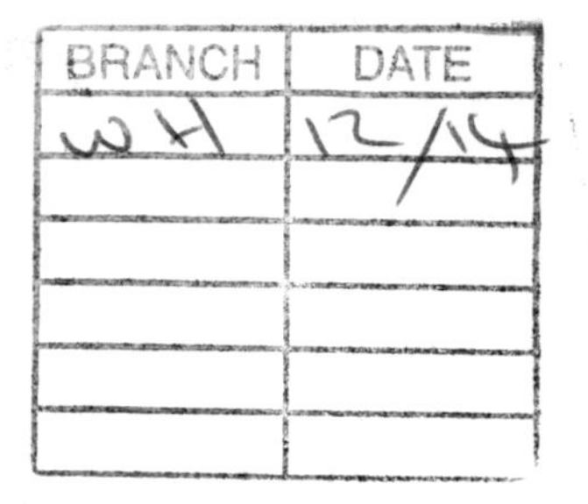
BRANCH
DATE